# MONEY TALKS –
## William Davis translates

*A Glossary of Money*

*Also by William Davis*

THREE YEARS HARD LABOUR
The Road to Devaluation

MERGER MANIA

# MONEY TALKS -
## William Davis translates

---

## A GLOSSARY OF MONEY

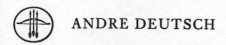 ANDRE DEUTSCH

First published 1972 by
André Deutsch Limited
105 Great Russell Street London WC1

Printed in Great Britain by
Ebenezer Baylis and Son Limited
The Trinity Press, Worcester, and London

ISBN 0 233 96254 9

# Author's Note

This book is arranged in alphabetical order, but to give a separate entry for every term you are likely to encounter would have made it a very long book with a lot of duplication. You will therefore find that many terms are included under a different heading, for example, under BALANCE SHEET you will find that I have dealt with RESERVES, CURRENT LIABILITIES, FIXED ASSETS, etc. It is therefore essential, if you are checking on a particular word or phrase, that you use the index first. It is also obvious that some of the subjects are very wide and come under different headings, for example under COMMON MARKET I have dealt with a whole range of subjects and you will also find the Common Market cropping up under other headings, like under AGRICULTURAL POLICY, TREATY OF ROME etc. I have included cross references where it seemed appropriate but the index is the key to successful use of the book.

Of course if you are not in a hurry you can simply read it straight through like any other book.

# Preambulatory Inception Brief[1]

'The point is that the thing for Mr Jenkins to think of, *inter alia,* in making his judgment, and for observers to have in mind in judging it, is the whole of the V-shape above the probable range of payments outcomes, not just its base or the intersection with the point of greatest probability'.

Peter Jay, Economics
Editor of *The Times.*

'The wider bands system therefore risks being either too rigid or too volatile. It may have a double disadvantage. It gives perhaps excessive immediate flexibility, with scope for "normal" variations in exchange rates that if left to themselves may be inappropriate for the desired correction of the payments balance, and yet involve significant uncertainty to traders and investors. At the same time, unless it leans significantly on parity changes which will introduce their own disturbances, it has inadequate continuing flexibility.'

Fred Hirsch, author of
*Money International.*

Do they *have* to talk like that? Is it impossible to discuss money in simple language? There are people who have made a million – and more – without ever finding out what wider band system, business cycle, progressive taxation, or contango mean. So, I suppose, the short answer is 'No'.

Every trade, or profession, has its jargon. Even the man whose life is devoted to selling baked beans will, on occasion, use words and phrases which outsiders do not understand. Scientists, including economists, have a particular strong case for using their own special language, their own precise modes of calculation and communication. Some things sound complex because they *are* complex. Jargon, moreover, offers comfort and security. It's safer to use terms accepted by fellow-experts than to lay oneself open to a charge of over-simplification. If outsiders want to enter one's world – well, let them learn the language.

[1] Foreword.

There is also the argument, of course, that you have to sound complex to impress. Economics is a comparatively young science, and economists have never been quite sure of their place in the academic and business worlds. Theirs is an inexact science, and there is a natural temptation to look down on it. At the universities, economists are often held in low regard. In business, they are frequently dismissed as day-dreamers who couldn't sell a pair of shoes, or run a company, in a month of Sundays. It's one reason why the jargon of economics is worse than most. It takes considerable skill, moreover, to keep up with it. There's an old joke, well known among economists, about the student who went back to his university, after twenty years, and found that the examination papers still asked exactly the same questions. 'Ah, but you see', his old professor explained, 'in economics the questions stay the same, but we change the answers.'

Economists themselves often make fun of their profession's lack of contact with reality. Milton Friedman, the Chicago economist, once told an appreciative audience of fellow experts the following story: 'A chemist, physicist and an economist were stranded on a desert island. They had nothing but canned food, and no can-opener. The chemist said that if they lit a fire, he could calculate the degree of heat needed for the cans to burst open. The physicist said that, if the chemist did that, he could calculate the trajectory of the food as it shot out of the can, so that they would be able to stand in the right place to catch it. The economist said he couldn't understand all the fuss. The answer was perfectly simple. "Let us *assume* we have a can-opener."'

Economists, of course, are by no means the only people who come in for this kind of mockery. Technocrats are every bit as good a target. Not long ago, a British college of technology circulated a tactical manual for use 'in the battles with technological and management whizzkids' among its 330 apparently hard-pressed staff. Describing itself as a guide in 'verbal one-upmanship' it consisted of thirty key nouns and adjectives deployable in conversation with technocrats. 'Take any word from the first column', the authors advised, 'combine it with any word in the second column – then add any word in the third column.' Here is the Guide:

8

| | | |
|---|---|---|
| Integrated | Management | Options |
| Total | Organization | Flexibility |
| Systemized | Monitored | Capability |
| Parallel | Reciprocal | Mobility |
| Functional | Digital | Programming |
| Responsive | Logic | Concept |
| Optical | Transitional | Time-phrases |
| Synchronized | Incremental | Projection hardware |
| Compatible | Third generation | Contingency |
| Balanced | Policy | Decision |

If the instructions are followed, the manual claimed, 'few listeners will admit ignorance of the impressive-sounding result'.

John Kenneth Galbraith, who has occasionally been attacked by his academic colleagues for writing too well, says[1] that clear and unambiguous statement may not be the best medium for persuasion. Had the Bible been in clear, straightforward language, he maintains, it would almost certainly have been a work of lesser influence. The archaic constructions and terminology put some special strain on the reader, so by the time he has worked his way through it all he has a vested interest in what he has read. A newspaper column is more easily dismissed. The ambiguities of the Scriptures, moreover, allow infinite debate over what is meant. I have great admiration for Professor Galbraith and I like to think he was joking, but I am sure that a lot of economists would go along with his argument. To me, though, this kind of reasoning is anathema. To defend economic jargon and ambiguity on the grounds that, in order to appreciate and accept another man's case, you must find it hard to understand seems to me pretentious nonsense.

Not only pretentious but, all too often, dangerous. Finance and economics are not just academic subjects, reserved for the cosy study or classroom. They do not exist to prove the validity of pet theories, but to serve the individual. Nor, for that matter, are they the exclusive preserve of an administrative élite. The days when people did as they were told have gone. A politician has to sell himself, and the theories of economists, to those whose cooperation is

[1] In his book *Economics, Peace and Laughter*.

A*

9

needed to make them work. You don't sell an incomes policy to the workers on the factory floor by publishing incomprehensible government papers, and lecturing them on wider band systems. The trade unions, particularly, tend to be in no mood to listen to jargon, however elegant. Governments rightly regard 'wage explosions' as a menace. To the worker, though, it's simply a matter of looking after your own interests. The 'corporate philosophy' is to maximize profits. Why shouldn't workers join managements in the race for bigger gains? You won't get them to change their minds unless you can convince them, in plain English, that the whole thing is certain to backfire. Bloodymindedness, fear, panic – these things cannot be measured by building economic models, yet they clearly have a major bearing in modern economic and business management.

There are, in addition, a great many people who are interested in economics by the fact that this vast area so obviously affects the fate of governments, and the future of their own jobs and business ventures. There is no reason why they should be fluent in the language of the specialist.

Many thoughtful economists accept that, in today's changed conditions, it's not enough to produce learned papers. They recognize that the very quality of post-war economics, the greater sophistication of its theoretical constructions, its much refined statistical methods, may have made economics more respected in the universities, but has tended at the same time to put it out of touch with real economic situations. Sir Alec Cairncross, a former head of the British Government's economic service, says that 'economists have been insulated from industrial and commercial problems, and encouraged to apply themselves to those fascinating conundrums in which pure theory is so rich'. And he has this warning for non-experts: 'Beware of being marched up in bold logic by the priestly up the garden path.'

His views are not, of course, shared by all of his colleagues. Some have shown increasing disgust with the whole democratic process: the mechanics of electioneering, the apparent stupidity of trade unions, and the reluctance of individuals to go along with schemes which, on paper, have obvious merits. These men have sought refuge in the sheltered, comforting surroundings provided by their universities. They argue that, if their schemes have not worked out as intended, it's all the fault of stupid politicians and an equally stupid electorate. Their advice to fellow-experts is to concentrate on refining economic theories, and to maintain a dignified silence.

This, of course, is much the safest approach. Pretend that economics has nothing to do with real life, and no one will ever give you trouble. There are, nevertheless, people who think economics has a little more to offer. 'It is not enough', says Cambridge's Graham Hallett, 'to have a good idea; the practical problems of implementing it must be carefully thought out if it is in practice to do more good than harm.' Any businessman could have told him that years ago, but it is nice to have it acknowledged.

The ideal solution, clearly, is for economists to acknowledge that their ideas must not only be practical but, as far as possible, to be comprehensible to the intelligent layman – and for the rest of us to make some effort to discover what it's all about. If this book helps, I shall be delighted. Its origins go back to my publisher's suggestion that I should write a guide to money which my Aunt Bertha could understand. Aunt Bertha is a fictional character I created for my column in *The Guardian* some years ago, as a way of making jargon understood by ordinary people. As it turned out, she quickly acquired a personality of her own, and started to express unorthodox, highly critical, views on economics and finance. Today she is a very real person to many *Guardian* readers – and, I confess, to me.

I have put together a glossary of terms used regularly by economists, specialists in international finance, accountants, financial editors, stock market dealers – and millionaires. I have deliberately included catch-phrases such as 'Yankees Go Home' and 'The Quality of Life', because they have had such wide currency. The overall aim has been not only to translate, but to get as close as possible to what I believe to be the practical meaning of a word or phrase. It means, very often, that my interpretation differs from the one generally accepted in the academic world. No matter; in economics, and in business, there is room for more than one version. If you are completely at home in the world of fixed parities, floating currencies, conglomerates, multi-nationals, invisibles, leads and lags, and crawling pegs you may enjoy quarrelling with mine. For those who want to delve more deeply, I have added a list of books which I personally have found not only useful, but enjoyable.

Inevitably, there will be terms which I have missed. No glossary can ever be complete, if only because the volume of jargon is still growing at an alarming rate. Entry into the Common Market and new industrial relation laws have both widened the scope. Embarrassingly high unemployment has lead to the creation of euphemisms like 'disemployed' and 'involuntary leisure'. And, of course, jargon is spreading rapidly into normal business fields.

Take 'management by objectives', which is being offered on a consultancy basis as though it were a new discovery or some breakthrough in technology. You've read the interviews. 'Since we turned over to management by objectives we have etc, etc.' All it means is that 'since we sat down and decided to find out what we had to do to make profits etc, etc'. Targets of achievement are as old as man, yet one has seen consultant recommendations which advise 'management by objectives' as a revolutionary policy which allows the consultant to extract high fees. There are others. Cost effectiveness, cost benefit, discounted cash flow, management by committee. Shops have become retail outlets, even when they are shops – which I accept they are not all the time. Workers' overalls are 'career apparel' or 'corporate clothing'. One gets a completely foreign language in the product development business and even more so in the advertising game. Many of us have sat through those over-long presentations of new products where someone starts with sententious pronouncements accompanied by slides projected on a large screen. It takes him half an hour to wade through a barrel of phrases like motivational research, consumer orientation, and aspirational undercurrents to say that his company thought they ought to bring out a new chocolate bar because they expect it to make money.

Much of this nonsense comes from America and is enthusiastically adopted because it provides a veneer of professionalism. It's impossible to stop it, but next time someone tries to dazzle you with science ask him to explain, in plain English, what he's talking about. The chances are that he doesn't know either.

# 'A' SHARES

Usually shares which don't carry a vote. (They're also known as non-voting shares, which is a much more honest description.) 'A' shares helped men like Clore, Fraser, and Wolfson to build their empires through takeover bids without losing control. A popular method of financing bids is to offer the other side shares rather than cash. If these shares have full voting rights, there's always a risk that the victim, or victims, will eventually gang up against you. 'A' shares prevent this: no matter how large your empire grows, you will always have the final say through your voting stock.

From an ordinary investor's point of view, 'A' shares have the advantage that they qualify for exactly the same dividend as the rest, but are often cheaper. The chief disadvantage is that you're usually left out of the highly profitable auction which goes on during a take-over fight. 'A' shares are nowadays frowned upon in the City, and many people feel they should be outlawed. Several major companies have enfranchised all their shareholders and there are comparatively few new issues of this type of stock.

# AD VALOREM

In business, as in law and sex, Latin words and phrases are some-times used instead of English. This is to make the subject look more dignified and authoritative. (In sex, of course, it is a way of dis-cussing the subject without actually mentioning the unspeakable: even Indian terms like *lingam* and *yoni* are acceptable.) *Ad valorem* means 'according to value'; an *ad valorem* tax (such as stamp duty) is one levied on a percentage of value. As far as I'm concerned, the English translation would do just as well – but that would, of course, mean breaking with tradition.

Other Latin phrases you may come across include *ex gratia* ('as a matter of favour'), *a fortiori* ('with all the more force') and *ad referendum*, a term sometimes used in connection with a contract, meaning that, although it has been signed, certain matters have been left over for consideration. There are other terms – indeed, one could go on *ad infinitum* – but they are not really vital to an under-standing of your business – unless, perhaps, you happen to be in the hands of a crooked lawyer.

13

## ANNUAL GENERAL MEETING

A yearly ritual imposed on public companies by law. The AGM is open to all shareholders, but the majority of meetings are sparsely attended and dreadfully dull. The British, on the whole, don't like complaining. It embarrasses them. So the chairman races through the agenda, accepts a vote of thanks, and rushes off to the nearest bar, relieved that the democratic process is over for another year. I have seen meetings disposed of before we've all had time to take our coats off: the legal formalities can be got through in a few minutes.

Once in a while, though, someone does make a bold attempt to hold up the proceedings. He may be a professional trying to exploit the occasion. Or a genuine, sensible chap representing a group of like-minded people. Or a crank. Cranks and eccentrics provide the most fun, though they often go too far. Midland Bank meetings used to be enlivened by a farmer in dirty gum boots, who harangued the board non-stop and, when they tried to terminate the meeting, leaped on the polished boardroom table and walked up and down hurling abuse at the directors. At their best eccentrics manage to puncture inflated boardroom egos. At their worst, they allow directors to uphold the British reputation for tolerance. Mostly they brighten up routine occasions.

One performer I remember with particular affection was an Irish spinster who wore the most outlandish clothes and turned up at meetings on a bicycle. At one meeting she propped up her cycle outside the door of the Dorchester and was haughtily refused admission. She eventually got in, asked many pertinent questions, and was treated with great respect by the rather terrified board. Her counterpart in America, cigar-smoking Mrs Stross, once arrived at a United Steel meeting in a Gay Nineties costume – 'dressed to match management thinking'.

And an American called Lewis Dusenbery Gilbert was greeted once at an AGM by the chairman with 'I wish you were dead'. Gilbert applied his wealth and time entirely to championing the rights of minority shareholders, and made a national reputation as the terror of the boardrooms. The directors of Columbia Broadcasting spoke for many fellow executives when they complained: 'We used to look forward to the AGMs. Now we anticipate them with dread.' When

Gilbert made his first appearance at the annual meeting of Ford, Henry Ford II – recognizing him sitting quietly among the other shareholders – pointed him out and said: 'We missed you the last six years, Mr Gilbert. We have been expecting you every year. We did not know what was wrong with us.'

In Britain, financial journalists have fond memories of the 'Gordon riots' – a succession of stormy gatherings at which shareholders and directors of Gordon Hotels hurled invective at each other with a fervour and skill that makes today's House of Commons clashes look like meal-times in a kindergarten. At an annual meeting of Sidney Flavel, in the late fifties, a shareholder threw something more solid – three eggs and one tomato. He later explained that this is 'the only way I can show my disapproval'. It wasn't the first time someone has reinforced his arguments in this way. There was, for example, a tough Yorkshire character who travelled to London for annual meetings. He always wore a cloth cap, and never took it off. On one occasion, after asking the chairman a number of questions and getting unsatisfactory answers, he stood on his chair, took off his cap, and hurled it at the unfortunate company chief. Seasoned reporters also treasure the moment when a chairman, furious at persistent interruptions from a stockbroker, picked up a shareholders' register and threw it at his tormentor.

This sort of violence is comparatively rare nowadays, but students and others with a grievance have discovered that, with reporters present, annual meetings are a good way of drawing attention to a protest. Firms with interests in South Africa, for example, now tend to find themselves harassed by anti-apartheid demonstrators. Another group well placed to score are trade unionists; a single share will usually buy admission and, as long as they don't lose their tempers, they can often squeeze concessions out of an embarrassed board.

There are times, of course, when shareholders are their own worst enemy. They shout down a man when they should be backing him. Companies naturally encourage this by packing their meetings with senior employees who act as boo-leaders. Some also announce, at the earliest possible opportunity, that there is free sherry or (if the year's results look particularly bad) champagne waiting for them in an adjoining room. It seems churlish to criticize such a generous board, and anyone who tries to keep people from free booze is regarded as a cad. (Another favourite trick is to hold your annual meeting in a tiny place, far away from the big cities, which no one has ever heard of and which shareholders and financial journalists have not the slightest desire to visit.)

But perhaps the biggest problem is that professional critics – stockbrokers, accountants, bankers and the like – frequently go over to the other side. Stockbrokers are sometimes silenced by a discreet offer of business. And it is not unusual for accountants and bankers who make a nuisance of themselves to be invited to join the board. In many cases, of course, this is the chief motive for making a fuss in the first place: it's a quick way to the top.

## ANNUITY
A means of ensuring that you have a regular income for the rest of your life. There are several different types of annuities, but the most common involves the payment of a lump sum in return for a fixed income each year for the rest of your life. Its appeal, obviously, is chiefly to people who have retired or are about to retire and the cost of the annuity depends on age, state of health, and other factors. The main advantage is that you know exactly where you stand. The main disadvantage is that inflation may erode the value of your income (that lump sum might have been better invested in ordinary shares, which offer some chance of keeping pace with inflation) and that you may die prematurely. It's possible to pay out £10,000 one year and be forced to join your ancestors the next, leaving the insurance company with a nice profit. If there is a heaven, which I doubt, there must be an awful lot of disgruntled angels who rue the day they ever heard of annuities. On the other hand, it's fun to beat the company to it. The prospect of making a profit on the deal does, you will agree, considerably increase the incentive to live to 120. (See also ENDOWMENT.)

## APPRECIATION
An increase in the value of an asset. Property and shares don't go up, they appreciate. There's no reason for this; it merely sounds more

16

elegant. It's very much part of that odd vocabulary which the Stock Exchange uses to enhance its respectability. Financial journalists often try to go still further. If you read the daily stock market report in *The Financial Times* (or listen to it on the radio) you will see that there are a dozen or more ways of saying 'up'. Shares may 'harden', 'edge higher', 'strengthen', or 'improve'. It means, as a rule, that they have put on very little. I spent a year, long ago, writing part of the FT's report and I remember how hard we tried to think up new words. I mean, how many times can you say 'edge higher' or 'strengthen' in one paragraph? The temptation to resort to puns was irresistible. Motor shares invariably 'accelerated' and cement shares 'hardened'. They still do.

## ARBITRATION
A word made famous by trade union officials who appear on television and announce: 'I won't submit to arbitration.' It means, very simply, a procedure by which people who are having an argument submit it to a third party for settlement. Disputes over wages and conditions of employment usually go to the Industrial Arbitration Board, better known under its old title of Industrial Court and part of the British labour scene since 1919. Reference may also be made to an independent arbitrator appointed by Whitehall. A lot of people think arbitration is an unwarranted interference with free market forces, and refuse to accept the arbitrator's judgment – unless, of course, it happens to favour their own case.

## ASSETS STRIPPING
Taking over a company and selling off – or stripping – most of its assets. These may be unwanted properties, machinery, or stocks of goods and raw materials. Firms tend to be more efficient in their use of assets than they were ten or twenty years ago (the take-over boom has acted as a powerful spur) but the scope for stripping still seems to be considerable. It calls for a sharp eye, discretion, and the ability to make an utterly realistic assessment of what a firm's assets are worth. Many economists argue that the strippers are financial hyenas whose activities are of little help to the community: they throw people out of work and reduce competition. Others maintain

17

that, by keeping potential victims on their toes, they perform a useful economic function.

Some strippers have proved spectacular failures, but there have also been some outstanding successes: Jim Slater is perhaps the best-known example of the latter. (See BALANCE SHEET.)

## AUDITOR

A financial referee whose job it is to examine a company's books and confirm that its accounts give a 'true and fair view' of its position. He may also be asked to inspect the records of non-trading organizations such as social clubs. Auditors are generally accountants appointed by the company's directors, who also fix their fee. And yet, they are in many ways the shareholders' champion. They are entitled to demand books, documents and correspondence, and to insist on detailed explanations. If the directors have been up to no good, the auditor is supposed to qualify his report in a suitable manner.

The auditors' statement is always included in a company's annual report, and although it is usually printed in annoyingly small type, it's well worth an investor's while to read it. Auditors are independent accountants, and failure to point out misbehaviour can lead to an action for professional negligence. But the temptation to close one's eyes may, occasionally, prove irresistible. And even if they are completely honest, there is always room for error because quite a lot has to be taken on trust. One of the main areas of company fraud, for example, is the valuation of stocks. These consist, as a rule, of raw materials and finished or unfinished products, and may be substantial. It is clearly impossible for an auditor to check every single item, down to the last postage stamp, and to decide what the total may be worth at any given moment. He can satisfy himself that proper methods of assessment have been used, and make personal spot checks. But since valuation is, like the calculation of profit, more a matter of opinion than a strict fact, it is virtually impossible to ensure 100% accuracy.

Club accounts are usually simpler, and irregularities much easier to detect. It's surprising how many clubs fail to keep proper records, and how often an officer dips into the till. One well-known method of fraud, known as 'teeming and lading', involves bar takings. The bar manager hands them to the treasurer once a month, and he is supposed to pay them into the bank. He may, however, delay doing so, and use the money to settle personal bills. This is not, of course, fraudulent in itself, but it's often the start of trouble. He may find himself unable, the following month, to make up the difference, or the temptation to repeat the exercise may be too strong. By the end of the financial year there's a considerable gap between the amount actually in the bank, and the amount which should be there. Sometimes the treasurer can bridge the gap by borrowing; sometimes he decides to run off with the lot. The obvious answer is for club officials to cross-check each others' activities right through the year. Many people, though, feel this would be an insult to someone who, after all, gives his services for free. The possibility of fraud doesn't occur to them until it's too late.

## AVERAGING
The 100 shares you've bought go down, right? You're still keen on them, so you buy another 100 at the lower level. You now hold 200 at an average price lower than the one you paid when you first took a fancy to this particular investment. That's called averaging. It means that the price doesn't have to go up by as much before you show a profit. The case for averaging is strongest when the shares are depressed by factors which are clearly temporary, and have nothing to do with their basic merit. They may, for example, suffer during one of those irrational bouts of jitters which affects all stock markets from time to time. But beware of over optimism. Averaging makes sense only if your original judgment was correct. Wishful thinking merely makes the situation worse. Averaging up, rather than down, usually makes better financial sense because it goes with the trend, rather than against it.

## BACKWARDATION
What happens when the price of something for immediate delivery rises above its price for future delivery. In other words, a backwardation tells us that the price is expected to come down. It applies chiefly in the commodity market, but you're also likely to come

across it on the Stock Exchange. (A backwardation also happens to be the term for a payment made by a 'bull' to a 'bear' for not insisting on delivery of shares sold by the former to the latter.) The ordinary investor is unlikely to have much to do with it – but it certainly is impressive to be able to announce to your fellow guest at a dinner party: 'I see the backwardation on copper has disappeared.'

## BAD DEBTS

An occupational hazard of business. Modern society cannot function without debt, and inevitably some of it goes bad. Restaurants and stores are frequent casualties, but anyone who extends credit to someone else is a potential victim. The only way to avoid bad debts is to refuse to lend money or give credit. Most firms make a provision for bad and doubtful debts, but if they're wise they also recognize potential traps and take as much care as possible not to fall into them.

Banks, who are perhaps more vulnerable than anyone else, have a carefully worked-out set of rules which, they believe, protect them as far as is humanly possible. They teach managers to avoid excessive lending on security values, to watch out for signs that customers are over-extending themselves, to recognize over-optimistic balance sheets, to beware of people whose fortunes depend too much on one trade customer, and to spot glib characters who know every facet of fraud and don't hesitate to make use of it. But so much depends on personal judgment – one's assessment of another man's character, ability, integrity, and prospects – that there must always be room for error. There are, moreover, factors beyond a customer's control, including floods and natural disasters for farmers, and sudden death or illness. Many sickly accounts can be nursed back to health by careful handling at the right time: it's dangerous to throw good money after bad, but there are many occasions when a little understanding is the best form of protection. The avoidance of bad debts is not necessarily and completely a proof of business acumen. It may simply be a sign of excessive timidity. Each lender, whether businessman or banker, must make up his own mind about the people he deals with. If in spite of all care and prudence, he still finds himself faced with the danger of loss, the principles of recovery come into play. The law is on his side, but this may not be enough: one usually succeeds in recovering only part of the original loan or debt.

## BALANCE OF PAYMENTS

An attempt to show the effects of financial transactions a country carries on with foreigners. Wrongly assumed to be a reliable barometer to its economic health. The balance of payments is no guide to economic performance or of productivity: a country can have a big payments surplus and a stagnant economy, as Britain did in 1971.

Key factors affecting the balance of payments are imports and exports, earnings from sources like insurance and shipping, and movements of capital between one country and the rest of the world. The latter, in particular, can fluctuate quite sharply. Half the infamous deficit 'inherited' by Mr Wilson in 1964, for example, was due to an over-rapid rise in private investment abroad, notably a huge Shell investment in Italy's Montecatini group. Another big influence is the inflow and outflow of so-called 'hot money' (see p. 102).

There is nothing sinful in a balance of payments deficit as such: if every country in the world tried to run a permanent surplus, international trade would dry up. But the ability to carry a sizeable deficit for any period of time depends on the strength of other assets. If an individual owns a house, and stocks and shares which can be readily turned into cash, no one will worry if he runs up an overdraft. It's the same with a country. Britain has formidable overseas assets, in the form of investments in shares and factories abroad, but most of these are privately owned and not readily available to the Government. It therefore has to rely chiefly on our 'liquid assets' – the gold and currency reserves (see p. 96). When these are low, foreigners tend to get worried about our ability to defend the existing exchange rate and withdraw their money. This happened under Mr Wilson's government. Many economists feel that Mr Wilson exaggerated the seriousness of the problem, and in so doing produced more trouble than necessary for both the Government and the country. They resent the fact that the payments deficit was presented as a vast political and moral issue, curable only if everyone worked twice as hard. The balance of payments, they say, is a pseudo problem, easily solved through greater exchange rate flexibility. (See also INVISIBLES.)

## BALANCE SHEET

A piece of paper which shows the financial position of a company at a specific date. On the left are liabilities, and these may include the following:

**Issued share capital:** the money put up by shareholders. Since it is mostly permanent capital, there is no repayment date. It cannot be suddenly withdrawn.

**Mortgages, debenture stock, loan capital:** this is borrowed money which may or may not, have a definite repayment date.

**Reserves:** these are profits which have been retained in the business, and therefore belong to shareholders. They may be revenue reserves (profits which originate from trading) or capital reserves (profits which arise from the sale of capital assets). It's largely a book-keeping item, because the money is being employed in the business.

**Current liabilities:** these include items which are more liable to fluctuation, such as bank overdrafts, money owed to the taxman, and trade creditors.

Assets are on the right-hand side of the balance sheet, and include the following:

**Fixed assets:** factories, machinery, transport, and other permanent fixtures, such as office property. They are employed for the purpose of running the business – not for re-sale. Most balance sheets show the cost and a more recent valuation; the activity of take-over bidders has made most boards mindful of the need to show up-to-date values.

**Goodwill:** a nebulous term, basically meaning the value put upon the company's reputation. It may have been around for a long time and be highly regarded in its industry, or it may have acquired subsidiaries at a very favourable price. Because goodwill is such an intangible item, it tends to be the subject of considerable debate among financial purists. Some think it should be excluded altogether; all agree that it complicates investment analysis.

Current assets: these are the assets held by the company with the object of converting them into cash. The most important categories are debtors' balances (money due from customers), cash and near-cash such as short-term loans and tax reserve certificates, and stocks and work-in-progress.

The surplus of current assets over current liabilities is known as the company's 'working capital'. It measures the extent to which it can finance any increase in turnover. If it's non-existent, watch out. It may be a sign of trouble.

Balance sheets are drawn up (the official work is 'struck') on a certain date. For this reason, they are a record of the past, and should not be seen as a reliable guide to the future. They are usually several months old by the time they are published. Major items in them may be quite misleading: variables like stocks, creditors, and overdrafts, may have changed considerably within a short period.

A balance sheet, moreover, does not always give a true picture even of the past. It shows how much money has been spent, but not whether it has been spent wisely. Fixed assets are a major item, and stock market analysts frequently stress the 'assets backing' for a share. But assets are only worth what they produce in terms of earnings. What use is a huge factory, entered at cost price, if it turns out goods which one can no longer sell at a profit? 'Goodwill' is another item which needs to be treated with suspicion. It is supposed to represent the value of the firm's reputation, but all too often it is simply a polite word for loss.

A balance sheet tells you nothing about market conditions, or about the quality of the management which runs the company. As the people who invested in Rolls-Royce know to their cost. (See also:

PROFIT AND LOSS ACCOUNT; ASSETS STRIPPING; DEBEN-
TURES; and WINDING UP.)

## BANK RATE
A device which, in many people's eyes, has the same effect on City
people as castor oil has on the rest of us – it makes them run. For
years now, television has used the same film shots of City messengers
rushing out of the Bank of England to spread the word that Bank
Rate has changed. No one really knows why, but there is a vague
feeling that Bank Rate is, somehow, of great national importance.
Officially, it is the rate at which the Bank of England will lend to the
banking system. But this means less to people than the widely held
belief that it sets the pattern for interest rates generally. The belief
is not without foundation, but Bank Rate is much less important
nowadays than it was, say, twenty years ago.

The Treasury still uses it to attract foreign money to Britain or
to prevent the withdrawal of funds which are already here. It also
makes use of Bank Rate as a weapon against inflation, particularly at
moments when reliance on the obvious alternative – higher taxes –
is politically inconvenient. But interest rates generally do not follow
Bank Rate in the way they used to. The building societies, for
example, are always quick to announce that Bank Rate changes do not
necessarily make any difference to their own policies. And now that
the clearing banks are competing openly for new deposits, individual customers may be offered rates which depart significantly
from Bank Rate. The latter is still useful as a broad indication of the
Government's line, and may be backed by all sorts of official
measures. There is no justification, however, for the popular
assumption that all other rates are automatically tied to it.

## BANKING REVOLUTION
A term used by financial journalists whenever the British banks –
once highly conservative – make an attempt to adapt themselves
to the twentieth century. Their move into hire-purchase and personal loans, the 'bank manager in your cupboard' commercials, the
cartoon films, the flashy ads in the colour supplements, and the
pretty Barclay-blondes in yellow Batman-type cloaks who pounced

on unsuspecting customers in off-licences to offer them free credit cards, were each billed as a 'banking revolution'. So was the decision, towards the end of 1971, to drop the old cartel arrangements on overdraft and deposit rates.

Until then, competition for deposits had been limited by a cosy gentlemen's agreement which kept interest down to a miserable 3%. The 1971 move amounted, on paper, to a declaration of war. But the banks balked at ideas developed much earlier in the United States and Japan. In the US, banks had wooed savers with offers of saucepans, luggage, clock radios, portable television sets and even Cadillacs. In Japan, they had given free traffic insurance, and made contributions to educational schemes, to everyone who agreed to deposit a reasonable sum of money for a reasonable period of time. The British banks, for all their new-found commercialism, frowned at this sort of stuff: they called it undignified and expensive. What they really meant, though, is that they were doubtful about the value of this sort of thing at a time of comparatively low economic growth. Let the Government go for fast expansion and, bingo, demand for more credit would lead to a 'new era' in competition for deposits.

## BANKRUPT
A person legally declared unable to pay his debts. The word is said to have originated in renaissance Italy, at a time when bankers and money-changers conducted their affairs from benches or stalls on the Italian bourse. When one failed or became insolvent, his bench was destroyed and the name *banco-rotto,* or 'broken-bench', was given to him. To the French, the word became *banqueroute*; to the English, banker-out. In time it became 'bankrupt'.

A bankrupt used to be treated as an outcast, and bankruptcy still has a certain stigma attached to it. But the sting is not nearly as sharp as it used to be. It no longer strikes a bankrupt in Britain as much of a hardship, for example, to be prevented from voting in the House of Lords or House of Commons. And it's a mistake to think that a bankrupt automatically loses everything. Both Britain and America allow certain exemptions.

More and more, bankruptcy is regarded as an acceptable way out of deep financial trouble, a way of wiping the slate clean. It isn't pleasant, of course, but it's better than stealing or having a nervous breakdown. Some people even argue that bankruptcy was originally derived from the Bible. They quote from the Revised Standard Version: 'At the end of every seven years you shall grant a release. And this is the manner of the release: every creditor shall release what he has lent his neighbour; he shall not exact it of his neighbour, his brother, because the Lord's release has been proclaimed.'

You can become a bankrupt by filing a petition with the court, or letting a creditor do so, together with a list of your assets and people to whom you owe money. In most cases the debtor has no assets and challenging him, in court, is not only a waste of time but tends to be expensive – since legal fees have to be paid.

You may apply for a discharge at any time after that, and whether you get it or not depends on whether the court thinks you have made sufficient effort to repay all or part of your debts.

Bankruptcy has increased tremendously in recent years, and one good reason is the comparative ease with which one can nowadays get credit. There have never been so many pressures on people to go in for instalment buying, or to borrow money. The bigger the temptation, the greater the likelihood of financial disaster. Many well-known people have, over the last decade, filed a petition for bankruptcy, without finding themselves condemned as sinners. George Sanders, Betty Hutton and Mickey Rooney all trooped through courts and survived. In the United States, people with large debts can opt for an alternative method of bankruptcy known as 'Chapter XIII'. Under this, he doesn't seek release from what he owes, but asks for an extended period of time to pay what he owes – usually three years. It probably amounts to the most realistic approach to the whole problem.

The only time a bankrupt finds himself in really serious trouble is when someone can prove that fraud is involved. Example: knowing that his business is failing, a fraudulent trader may order goods to the maximum that his credit will stand – and then 'give' them to a friend or relative or transfer them to a source from where he can recover them when he's ready to start up in business again. You'd be surprised how many people try this sort of thing and how few get away with it.

# BARGAIN
Stock Exchange deals are always known as bargains – a cunning attempt to make investors believe that they've done well for themselves. Someone once said that a bargain is something so reasonably priced that they won't take it back when you find out what's wrong with it. That doesn't happen on the Stock Exchange, but take care not to be seduced by the word. When I was on *The Financial Times*, many years ago, we had a letter from an old lady in Bournemouth who complained bitterly that the dozen or so shares she had bought on our recommendation were all showing a loss. We couldn't trace any record of the recommendations, and wrote to her to say so She replied that we were having her on: surely we knew the paper printed a daily section, among all the other prices changes, headed 'special bargains'? The section, of course, simply recorded deals which did not fit under any of the normal headings, and no expert could possibly have been fooled by it. But we're not all experts!

# BASLE CLUB
One of Europe's most influential conclaves. Officially known as the Bank for International Settlements, it was conceived in the late 1920's as part of an attempt to 'take finance out of politics'. The bank was founded by leading European central banks, and is, essentially, a meeting ground of central bank governors.

Once a month, they get together in the Euler or Schweitzerhof hotel for a weekend of informal talks, with just a perfunctory official session with other BIS officials. Politicians are neither invited nor welcome. The Basle Club has been described as 'essentially a team of maintenance men, trying to keep the mechanism of the international monetary system humming smoothly'. It is an apt description. They are the experts who know how the machinery works, but ultimately it's the politicians who make the key decisions. Central bankers usually try to get on with their political masters, but are very much aware that the need to win public favour may lead to departures from financial orthodoxy. They can recommend a certain course of action, but the final say lies with the finance ministers of each country. Not surprisingly, this often leads to friction. The most widely publicized clash of recent years has been that between Mr Harold Wilson and Lord Cromer, Governor of the Bank of England when Labour won power in 1964: when his Lordship's term was up the Government decided to replace him with someone they thought less hostile. Similar clashes have taken place in other countries, notably Germany and the United States. And yet, the Basle Club has often bailed out politicians when they appear to be in trouble. When Labour hit its first financial crisis, shortly after the 1964 election, Lord Cromer telephoned each of his fellow club members and within twenty-four hours put together a $3,000 million loan. It was impressive proof of the Club's ability to act quietly, and secretly, when the need arises.

More recently, it has been an important forum for discussing such questions as sterling's role as a reserve currency, the future of gold, and greater exchange rate flexibility. The so-called Basle Agreement resulted largely from its deliberations. No central banker can ignore the fact that politics play a big part in the Capitalist Way of Finance – but the Basle Club, meeting so close to where the Gnomes of Zürich allegedly plot the downfall of the system, does its best to see that political fancy is turned into the bankers' idea of down-to-earth, realistic, matter-of-fact policy.

## BEAR

Someone who sells stocks he doesn't own in the hope that he can buy them at a lower price before delivery is due. The term is also applied, generally, to those who take a pessimistic view of the future: they are said to be 'bearish'.

A bull is exactly the opposite – someone who buys shares in the hope of the price going up. And in the same way, to be 'bullish' is to feel optimistic about the future.

A 'bear market' is one which has seen a prolonged fall in prices, and which does not look capable of a sustained recovery.

A concerted attack by speculators is known as a 'bear raid'. People are selling a share, or a currency, which they haven't got, hoping that the price will fall. They then move in, buy at the lower level, cover their commitment, and pocket the difference. A 'bear squeeze' is exactly the opposite; prices are forced up, and the share or currency which the bears need to clear their commitments is withheld, so that the bears have to pay heavily.

## BEGGAR-MY-NEIGHBOUR

Selfishness in trading partners; one country following restrictive policies at the expense of another. Governments are always tempted to protect themselves from foreign competition through high tariffs and other measures, and there have been periods when protectionism has been fashionable almost everywhere. The astonishing growth in world trade over the past few decades owes much to a widespread awareness, among Western industrial nations, that this sort of thing can backfire. If one country pulls down the shutters, there is nothing to stop the others from doing the same. Supra-national institutions like the International Monetary Fund are pledged to fight for free trade, and the United States has been remarkably liberal since the last world war. In Britain, the refusal of the 1964–70 Labour Government to have anything to do with import quotas – putting a limit on the quantity of foreign goods allowed into the country – was chiefly due to fears of retaliation. Nevertheless, protectionism is on the increase. The Americans, in particular, have become impatient – strong political pressure groups in Washington frequently stress that Japan's restrictive trade policies, and arrangements such as the EEC's Common Agricultural Policy, call for an effective answer. Any major move towards 'beggar-my-neighbour' policies would be a blow for countries which depend on exports to keep their balance sheet straight. This includes Britain – and, worse, most of the developing countries.

## BEHAVIOURAL SCIENCE

Attempts to find out not only what men do, but why they do it. Behavioural scientists are increasingly used by organizations to help with management problems – to identify talent, improve leadership, raise the level of communications, and reduce wastage of human effort. It's a worthy cause, because it recognizes that business success depends on more than facts and figures. Dozens of books have been published on the subject, especially in the United States, and most of them are well worth reading. Inevitably, though, behavioural scientists themselves are often so fascinated by the theoretical side of their studies that they move away from reality. And, of course, they have developed their own jargon: they talk of 'self-actualization' (know yourself, and make the most of your talents) and 'insightful management'.

A London business school student, not long ago, injected a badly needed touch of humour into the whole business by suggesting that the dramatic works of Shakespeare, commonly supposed to have been written simply for the theatre, were in fact originally used as case studies in organizational behaviour. In case No 20 (*Romeo and Juliet*) 'we see the harmful effects of a breakdown in communications between two organizations in an oligopolistic context. This situation is not rectified until informal inter-organizational communications have been set up at an employee level, with disastrous results'. Case No 26 (*Hamlet*), the student added, was about 'a highly sophisticated young executive who was quite unable to make decisions at all'. Shakespeare, clearly, was well ahead of his time: it's a pity that modern behavioural scientists can't write so entertainingly.

## BIG BOARD
The popular term for the New York Stock Exchange, by far the largest and most influential stock market in the US. The next largest market is the American Stock Exchange, popularly known as the 'Amex', which specializes in smaller, up-and-coming companies. There are stock exchanges in many other cities, including Boston, Detroit, Cincinatti, and San Francisco, which make a market in local corporations, and in stocks already listed on the Big Board. There's also a huge and important over-the-counter market, which is not really a single market at all but a collection of dealers scattered all over the country.

## BLUE-CHIP
Originally an American term, now widely used in Britain. It means 'a high-quality ordinary share', and derives from a gambling chip – the highest valued are coloured blue. Stocks which qualify for this coveted label have usually been favoured by investors for many years and are established market leaders. They are less risky than

some of the most adventurous stocks (known as 'high-fliers') but it's a mistake to assume that, just because they have a fancy name, they must be loss-proof. Their very success may be against them; they may have reached heights where dynamic growth is a thing of the past. Rolls-Royce was a blue-chip. Timing, moreover, is just as important with blue-chip stocks as with everything else. A market leader like ICI is more sensitive to adverse national news, such as a balance of payments setback or a tough Budget, than many a small company. And there may be periods when investors' enthusiasm has run too far ahead of actual performance. As any market chart will show you, the price of ICI and other blue-chips fluctuates quite considerably during the course of any year. If you buy at the wrong moment, you may lose money, blue-chip or not.

## BOARD MEETING
An event designed to make company directors feel important. Someone once said that many board meetings are held each month for no better reason than that it's been a month since the last one. It isn't the whole story. A great many more are held because they impress the rest of the office, and because they save directors the embarrassment of having to make tricky decisions on their own. At every meeting there is at least one character who obviously hates the idea of returning to his desk. So he takes a molehill and expertly develops it into a mountain. He asks questions, raises points, requests additional data, demurs and delays. He covers indefinite ideas with infinite words. And at the end of it he suggests another meeting. Of course.

The passion for meetings is dangerous, as well as tiresome, because it frequently harms relationships which have been carefully built up over the years. You may lose your temper, in the heat of debate, or alienate valuable allies by taking their opponents' side in a particular argument. You may commit frightful indiscretions, lose face, and even find yourself goaded into the ultimate folly – resignation. It all gets jotted down in 'minutes': the chap who thought up that one had a sense of humour.

People with multiple directorships are sometimes so hard pressed that they forget which company's board meeting they are at. One well-known property developer, Harry Jasper, held 400 directorships at the height of his career. One effective way of avoiding this kind of trap is to refuse ever to serve on a board. Another is to give your secretary explicit instructions on how to avoid getting you involved in meetings. The next time someone telephones to ask you to come to a meeting, get her to purr sweetly and say: 'Sorry, he can't. He's in a meeting.'

## BOILER ROOM OPERATION

Wall Street jargon for efforts to sell stocks over the telephone. In a typical boiler room there are rows of desks with nothing but telephones on them. Each will be manned by a fast-talking salesman who will try to sell highly speculative stocks (in other words, stocks of questionable value) to over-eager members of the public. The answer is simple: hang up. No matter how persuasive the voice at the other end, no matter how easy it sounds to make a quick killing, the gullible buyer will usually end up the loser. Some firms also offer bargain stocks by mail; millions of dollars are lost each year in this way.

## BOND

An IOU issued by a government, local authority or company as a promise to repay money over a period of time. People buy bonds to get the interest paid on them – the same way people put money in banks to get interest. Bonds with less than five years to run are usually called short-dated; those with a life of between ten and twenty years are medium; those with a life of more than twenty are long. Bonds may also be undated or irredeemable (in other words, not terminable by repayment) and some companies issue convertible bonds – meaning they can be converted into a fixed number of shares of its common (or 'ordinary') stock at some future date. The attraction of the 'convertible' is that it offers the security of a fixed income, plus the chance of a profit if the common stock into which the bond is convertible should go up in market value.

## BRETTON WOODS

A town in New Hampshire, USA, where forty-four nations decided, in July 1944, to set up a new international monetary system. The previous system had been based on the so-called Gold Standard, but it collapsed in the 1930s. The confusion and growth in nationalistic policies which followed highlighted the need for an entirely new system. Plans had been drawn up some time before, and the Bretton Woods Conference was called to discuss details. Among the delegations were representatives of most of the Allies, including the Soviet Union and other East European countries; nations of the British Empire; and Western European and Latin American countries. Many of them were unhappy with Anglo-American domination of the conference, and the Soviet Union announced that it would not take part in the new system.

British economist John Maynard Keynes, one of the key figures at the Conference, suggested the creation of an international bank, which could grant credits to its members. The credits, in the form of a new international currency called the *bancor* would be given to nations on the basis of their pre-war share of world trade. America vetoed the idea (chiefly because Britain stood to gain more than the US) but agreement was reached on the creation of two new institutions. One, the World Bank, was intended to provide loans to developing nations and to countries whose economies had been severely damaged by the war. The other, known as the International Monetary Fund, was given responsibility for supervising the system. (See WORLD BANK AND INTERNATIONAL MONETARY FUND.)

# BROKER

*The Concise Oxford Dictionary* says he's a 'dealer in second-hand furniture, etc'. The brokers I know in the City would have a fit if they knew; it sounds so desperately undignified. But the word covers a multitude of jobs, all of which come down to the same thing – a broker is a middleman. There are bullion brokers, insurance brokers, foreign exchange brokers and (yes!) furniture brokers. Stockbrokers count themselves the aristocrats of the profession, and indeed this is how the public tends to see them. They are, essentially, agents for investors.

If you want to buy or sell shares on the Stock Exchange, you contact a broker. The Stock Exchange itself will supply a list, but most people go on personal recommendation – just as they do with lawyers and accountants. The broker takes your order and goes to see a jobber. A jobber is a member of a Stock Exchange who deals in stocks, and is not allowed to do business directly with the public. Your broker asks him to quote a price, without disclosing whether he's a buyer or a seller. The jobber will give him two; the lower one is the price at which he will buy, and the higher one at which he will sell. The margin between them is known as the jobber's turn: it is the main source of his income. The broker will charge you a commission on the deal: that's *his* main source of income. In practice, both tend to be quite smart operators on their own account, and are naturally well-placed to take advantage of conditions. They are on the spot, they know the game, and they are in a position to act quickly. There's no guarantee that your broker will always be absolutely honest. Some have been known to take orders in the morning, buy, watch the shares rise smartly in the afternoon, sell at a profit, and tell the client that they never bought the shares because they felt it was the wrong moment to do so.

My first job was with a stockbroking firm and I sometimes wonder what would have happened if I had stayed with it. One reason why I didn't was that, at the time, you had no real chance of making good unless you had lots of rich friends. I didn't. The Stock Exchange disapproved of advertising (it was, and still is, part of the pretence that stockbroking is an honourable profession rather than a trade) and new business was introduced through regular contact with the wealthy set. You didn't have to know much about investment; the main thing was to know the right people. Today firms are bigger and better organized, and stockbroking is no longer an exclusive club. The able young chap from grammar school, or a red-brick university, has a better chance of making good than he has ever had before. He doesn't even have to be a Tory; several stockbrokers I know support the Labour Party.

## BUDGET

In business, an attempt to lay down a blueprint for future operations. The system varies from firm to firm, but it is common for the directors to devise a master budget, and to ask each department to provide one of their own. Departmental heads try to predict their probable income and expenditure during the coming year, and submit their budgets to the Board. Forecasts, alas, often go wrong and in a well-run company regular comparisons are made between budgeted results and actual achievement. Minor deviations don't really count, but any major gap ought to lead to a thorough reappraisal. A common fault is over optimism about sales, and an under-estimate of costs. The remedy is swift, realistic action but it's surprising how often the top management decides to condone, or even to endorse, what has clearly turned out to be a piece of wishful thinking.

In government, budgets are an exercise which has to take place at least once a year because, without it, the civil service would not have official authorization to spend our money. Some people argue that the accounts should be circulated to MPs in advance, as most companies do with their shareholders, and that we should dispense with the showbiz part of the Spring Budget. Chancellors agree that the showbiz element has probably been overdone, and that modern economic management calls for more than a single, annual adjustment. This is why, nowadays, we tend to have so many 'mini-budgets'. But they also argue, rightly, that the Spring Budget is important because it's the one time in the year when the Government can introduce fundamental tax reforms. Indeed, it seems fair to claim that this is now a much more significant feature of the April Budget than ups and downs in purchase tax and interest rates. A penny or two off beer, and a modest reduction in the tax on cars and washing machines, isn't so marvellous when you know that it will almost certainly be offset, before long, by other price increases. Reforms, on the other hand, tend to be both far-reaching and permanent.

Paradoxically, cheerful budgets are often a sign that economic management has gone awry. One of the functions of a budget is to regulate spending, and the Treasury is much more likely to put money in our pockets when trade is poor, and unemployment high, than it is when everything seems to be going well. In other words,

35

chancellors distribute largesse when times are bad and punish us when they are good.

## BUFFER STOCKS

Scheme designed to iron out fluctuations in the price of raw materials, or to ensure continuity of supply. Bad weather, disease or some other adverse factor may, for example, substantially reduce production of rubber, cotton, or tea in a particular year. The normal market response would be for prices to rise sharply. (In practice, alternative sources of supply are often available.) A buffer stock scheme would help to prevent this. It may be operated by the government or by the industry itself, and it involves building up a stockpile of raw materials which can be used, when necessary, to bridge the gap.

As a rule, the people operating such a scheme fix a 'ceiling' and a 'floor' price. When prices reach the ceiling, they sell from their stockpile. When they drop to the floor, they buy the raw material (or 'primary product' as some experts insist on calling it) and add it to the hoard. It's much the same method as that normally applied in currency markets, where stocks of gold and foreign paper money are used to keep exchange rates within certain defined limits. It sounds fine in theory, and has been successfully used to prevent unwanted booms and slumps. But it clearly works only in the case of materials which can be stored at relatively little cost. The creation of an artificial market, too, may have unfortunate long-term effects. It is certainly open to abuse: buffer stocks tend to be operated more in the interests of producers than consumers.

## BUILDING SOCIETY

One of our most useful institutions, frequently criticized at home but envied abroad. They are non-profit making, a fact which is not as widely known as it deserves to be. Building societies are owned by their 'members' (their investing and borrowing customers), so they try to charge their borrowers the lowest rate that will provide interest to investors, management expenses, tax and a sum for reserve. There's an official government watchdog with the delightfully old-fashioned title of 'Registrar of Friendly Societies', but serious abuse is rare. No society has failed since the law was tightened up by a new Act in 1960.

Critics maintain that building societies tend to be too conservative, and perhaps a bit too fond of banquets and imposing office blocks. A common accusation is that they are quick enough to raise interest rates to home buyers when rates in general are going up, but irritatingly slow to respond when things go the other way. It's true enough, but where would home buyers be without them?

Investors can open an account at any branch, or by post. (It's useful to place money with a society which allows its branches to pay withdrawals quickly.) There are, in fact, two types of account – 'shares' and 'deposits'. The shares are not dealt in on the Stock Exchange and carry a rate of interest which may be varied from time to time. It's usually a shade higher ($\frac{1}{4}\%$ to $\frac{1}{2}\%$) than you will get on a deposit account because technically there's a slightly greater element of risk. If anything goes wrong with a society, depositors have first claim on its assets. Most societies are so strong, these days, that the distinction is really academic. But some people prefer to go for 100% safety. I have always thought it more important to stress two other factors. One, deal with a society which has 'trustee status', meaning that it measures up to government standards, or at least make sure that it belongs to the Building Societies Association. Two, check your tax position. Because interest is paid net of tax (in other words, with tax already deducted) the rate offered is not attractive to people who are not liable to tax. They could do better elsewhere. Surtax payers have also found, over the years, that building society investment is not always the most suitable.

## BUSINESS CONFIDENCE

The general state of opinion among businessmen at any given time. Said to be 'a tender plant', easily damaged if a politician says the wrong word. Actually, it depends on a great many factors – the state of world trade, the prospects for economic growth at home, the availability of credit, the willingness (and ability) of customers to place new orders and pay for those already executed, the views of friends and colleagues, and the amount of gin and tonic inside a

37

businessman at the precise moment when he is asked for his opinion.

Various organizations attempt to measure business confidence from time to time, but the result is almost invariably unreliable. This is partly because confidence varies from industry to industry, and from firm to firm. The chief reason, however, is that so many people lie. Their answer may be influenced by dislike of whatever government is in power, or by their eagerness to blame 'general conditions' for their own lack of success. The average company report reads something like this: 'The Government has got the country into a terrible mess, industry is fed up and depressed, there is no incentive to do anything, prospects are bleak – *and our profits this year are forty per cent up.*'

Some businessmen think it's good policy to sound optimistic; optimism is infectious. Others think it's better not to let the other fellow know that you are doing well. If he is a customer, he might insist that you bring prices down. If he's a business contact or a supplier in trouble, he might try to get a loan. All such embarrassment can be avoided by the simple device of telling your hard-luck story before the other fellow gets a chance to do so. In America, not long ago, three Lebanese brothers became famous as 'the crying Adjimmis' because they carried this to its obvious conclusion. They bought shoddy, dirt-cheap goods, advertised a 'closing down sale', and howled like a force nine gale about the cruel fate which was compelling them to put 'expensive quality goods' on the market at bargain prices.

Businessmen who run large corporations, with a quote on the stock market, will tell you that it's usually best to err on the side of caution in one's assessment of prospects. If you make an optimistic forecast, stockholders won't thank you, a year later, if it proves to have been justified. They are, after all, merely getting what you led them to expect. And God help you if things go wrong! A cautious forecast, on the other hand, gives you a good chance of being hailed as a hero if profits turn out to be better. It will all be attributed to the excellence of management; governments only collect blame, not credit.

The most dismal people I know are shipowners. A few years ago

I found myself on a luxury yacht, sailing towards Athens. My hosts were members of two of the wealthiest Greek shipping families. We drank gallons of *Dom Perignon* at breakfast and nibbled whitebait served by white-jacketed flunkeys. At noon we switched to caviar and *Chateau Lafite*. This, I said, is the life. While we were eating, we discussed business. My hosts seemed deeply depressed. Shipping, they confided, was in a frightful state. Everyone was losing pots of money. Prospects were grim. Guiltily, I spent a whole three seconds toying with the idea of saying no thank you, I won't have another portion of caviar. Then I remembered what one of their fraternity, Basil Mavroleon, had told me years before: '*Shipowners are always complaining. And when they die they leave a fortune.*'

## BUSINESS CYCLE

Also called trade cycle. It means alternating periods of ups and downs in business activity. Economists hold that the cycle is a continually recurring phenomenon of any business order, divided into characteristic phases. A typical cycle is made up of a period of expansion, a downturn or recession, a period of contraction, and an upturn or revival. The whole process used to last between five to ten years, but since the last world war cycles have been considerably shorter. The subject is highly complex: all sections do not turn up and down at the same time, and no two cycles are ever identical. There is no shortage of schemes for reducing swings in the economy, and governments spend much time and energy trying to smooth out ups and downs. The cycle has lost much of its old terror – but it has certainly not disappeared altogether.

## BUSTED BONDS

Loans to foreign governments who have stopped paying interest due on them, and in many cases have failed to honour their commitment to repay the issue at a later date. This is a highly specialized market and one in which the speculative element predominates. Some are issues of South American states and cities which are partially or entirely in default, and others are bonds issued many years ago by countries now under communist control. Pre-Revolution Russian Government bonds are well to the fore, along with Hungarian,

39

Rumanian, and Baltic bonds. From time to time, some or all of these enjoy a revival of interest. It is usually sparked off by news of some move towards *rapprochement* between the communist and capitalist worlds; there is always someone ready to believe that in order to gain some trade advantage the communists will be willing to settle debts incurred by people they threw out of office several decades ago. The revival usually tends to be short-lived. Many busted bonds are also known as 'lampshade bonds', because they do tend to make rather pretty lampshades!

## BUY BRITISH
Allegedly a fine way to demonstrate your love for Britain. A phrase much loved by the *Daily Express,* which has run several 'Buy British' campaigns over the years, and occasionally taken up by politicians. Usually taken out of the mothballs, and dusted down, whenever the pound is said to be 'in trouble'. The idea is to narrow the trade gap, and therefore help the balance of payments, by buying fewer foreign goods. In 1968, Czech-born Robert Maxwell, then an MP, ran a 'Buy British' campaign following an attempt by five Surbiton typists to demonstrate their patriotic fervour by working half an hour extra every day for free. Mr Maxwell argued that Buying British made more sense. Retailers cooperated by clearly marking certain goods with the Union Jack. The campaign was popular for a time, because it made ordinary people feel that they could do something to help. It inspired a whole range of other ideas, most of them dotty. One man wanted people to collect 'useless gold trinkets' – old wedding rings, watches and gold teeth – and take them to a specially created government purchasing centre. Another, the managing director of a small company, persuaded his staff to pay overtime earnings into a national fund, out of which was to be financed the conversion of 'an old obsolete aircraft carrier which has been lying moored up unused for twenty years into a floating overseas exhibition for Britain'. Many people sent cheques and postal orders to the Treasury. The whole thing petered out after a few weeks, as it deserved to do.

As an answer to market pressures on sterling, of course, 'Buy British' is no more effective than old wedding rings and postal orders. It is, at best, a touching gesture, and at worst an invitation to foreign trading partners to hit back with similar moves. The fault, however, lies not so much with ordinary people as with governments which make a moral issue out of a fixed exchange rate.

## CAPITAL
Can be any asset which earns money, or which could be sold on the open market. If you own a house, that's capital. If you run a business, stocks of raw material or half-finished products may be capital. But it is usual to draw a distinction between assets which you cannot easily dispose of and those which are readily available. The excess of current (i.e. readily saleable) assets over current liabilities is known as one's working capital.

It's amazing how much difference a little capital can make to a young man's career. It allows him to choose between wage slavery and independence, gives him self-confidence, and widens his horizon. The sum does not have to be very large. Hundreds of prosperous companies were started on modest army gratuities after the Second World War. And many young men who left the parental nest with a business 'dowry' have quickly achieved fame and fortune. If I were a millionaire, I reckon I could get both satisfaction and profit from backing able and ambitious young men – and taking a share stake in return. Alas, I'm still a little short of my first million. About £980,000 short, at a rough guess.

I'd rather not say anything about my working capital.

## CAPITAL GAINS TAX
A tax on profit as distinct from income – 'profit' meaning, in this case, any increase in the value of an asset. It could be shares, or a painting, or a second house. (Your first owner-occupied property is exempt, along with gains from football pools and gambling generally, savings certificates, premium bonds, defence bonds, and life assurance policies.) In practice, the tax is difficult to administer and widely evaded. It brings in a comparatively modest amount of revenue. Tax inspectors have the legal right to inspect the books of, say, a stockbroker and occasionally bring test cases to frighten the general body of investors. But it's a daft tax, on the whole, owing

more to political than economic motives. The objective is to attack private wealth and capital. Ironically, the first capital gains tax was introduced by a Conservative Government. Mr Selwyn Lloyd, then Chancellor, wanted to buy the cooperation of trade unions in a 'wage policy' and thought that one very good way of doing it would be to slap a further tax on unearned income. It didn't stop the unions from asking for more money, but when the Labour Government won power in 1964 it quickly extended the Tory tax: gains disposed of within twelve months were treated as ordinary income, and long-term gains were taxed at a flat rate of 30%. Mr Heath's Government has changed some of the provisions (the distinction between short-term and long-term has gone), but the tax itself remains – proving, once again, that once politicians of either side have discovered a new way of taxing the electorate they are most reluctant to let go.

## CAPITAL INVESTMENT

Investment in new plant and machinery. One of the key factors in economic growth; it's modern equipment more than an extra hour's hard work by individuals, which makes a country progress. In Germany, after the Second World War, businessmen had to buy new plant and machinery because the old lot was destroyed by allied bombs and guns. In Japan, industrialists learned from the Americans that modern equipment is the surest way to high productivity and fast economic growth. In Britain, we made do with old plant and machinery because it was there, because it was intact, and because trade unions were suspicious of anything that looked like change. We might have got away from this but for the fact that constant financial crises prevented fast economic growth, and forced companies to rely on out-dated, but undamaged, equipment. The ideal climate for investment is a booming, rapidly growing economy. Strong demand presses upon physical capacity, and makes firms want to expand. High profits give them the means to do so. This is a much more important factor than allowances or grants.

Some economists argue, with good reason, that Britain made things worse by continuing to invest heavily abroad – a hangover from the Empire days. The Labour Government tried to change

this, by introducing a tax system which penalized overseas investment, but the rate of investment at home remained disappointing.
'We are', Mr Wilson once said, 'a low investment industrial nation
and we ought to be high one. It is no exaggeration to say that the
whole future of this nation rests on it becoming a high investment
power.' He was right – but diagnosis, clearly, is easier than cure.

## CARAT SCALE

A way of defining the amount of other metal – often silver –
alloyed with gold. (Because pure gold is too soft and liable to wear
to be used extensively in jewellery, it is generally alloyed with
other metals.) Pure gold is 24 carat. In the United States jewellery is
usually 10 (in other words, just over 40% pure gold), 14 or 18 carat;
if you can afford to shop at Tiffany's, you will also find 22-carat
jewellery. In Britain the lowest standard accepted is 9 carat (which
accounts for more than three-quarters of the gold trade) with the
range extending through 14, 18 and 22 carat. In America the popularity of fraternity pins and other award emblems accounts for a vast
production of 10-carat alloys. In both countries, careful watch is
kept on all gold production, and every article is stamped with a
mark guaranteeing the declared gold content. Unlike the British,
however, American producers are allowed a leeway of half a carat
either way.

## CASH FLOW

A term you simply must know if you want to have a conversation
with accountants. Take cash in hand at the beginning of a year, add
to it the profit you've made less tax and dividends paid, add depreciation (which is a cost, but not an outlay, and therefore available
for a company's use) and, for good measure, whatever funds you've
managed to raise during the year. There you have your 'cash flow'.
It's a way of measuring what cash has gone through your fingers,
but of course any proper measurement has to take note of the use
you've made of it. Accountants like to make a distinction between
funds applied in everyday business and those used to buy permanent
assets. When they talk of the latter, they like to use the phrase 'discounted cash flow'. It's really an attempt to put a value today on a

flow of income in future years: in short, to assess the value of 'jam tomorrow'. If, for example, you buy another company you take the cost of your purchase, less tax and investment allowances, and estimate the profit (less tax) it will give you over the period of its life. The trouble with this kind of exercise, of course, is that things seldom remain the same. Accountants accept this, but argue that it beats relying on pure guesswork.

## CHARACTER TEST

Every senior executive's idea of jolly, sadistic fun. The basic principle is simple: you lure people into embarrassing situations to see how they make out. The late Lord Beaverbrook – this is a true story – once invited a City Editor (who shall be nameless) to go on a trip to Canada with him. During a long train journey, he initiated the kind of drinking contest which, given the old man's skill with bottle and glass, no one could hope to win. After four hours of solid imbibing, the poor City chap was in a complete stupor. Beaverbrook rose without a word, staggered to his compartment, and fell asleep. The next morning the lord's wrath was awesome to behold: the City Editor, utterly bewildered, was dispatched home to England, and thereafter Beaverbrook always scornfully referred to him as 'the man who gets drunk on trains'.

The most dangerous time, in Britain, is the Christmas party season. Managing directors hold parties not, as is commonly supposed, to reward their staff for a year's good work, but to see how well they can hold their liquor. The widely held view that Christmas is the season of goodwill is a myth: it is, more than anything else, the season in which skilful operators identify and eventually eliminate their victims. An astonishingly large number of people, misled by the smile on the face of the office tiger and by the deliberately engineered atmosphere of conviviality, discard the caution they have displayed all the year, and walk straight into the trap.

Above all, they say things to superiors, and even to rivals, which ought to remain unsaid. They score off a rival (or imagine they do) by putting him down in front of a couple of silly, but pretty, office girls. They embarrass a close colleague by giving everyone details of his private life. And they try to look big by making disparaging remarks about the chairman; remarks which, of course, are immediately reported back to him. A whole year's climbing may, in this way, be set back by an extra gin and tonic. The wisest approach to an office party is to work out a strategy in advance: put down all the things you want to say, the things you know are guaranteed to impress. Drink only tonic water; you can switch to stronger stuff *at home* later on. Be relaxed, but in complete control. Don't say a word more than you planned to say. Remember that, when another executive pats you on the back, he is merely calculating where to stick the knife.

## CHEAP MONEY

Money available at a low rate of interest. From 1932 until 1951 successive British governments deliberately kept interest rates down; apart from a few weeks in 1939, Bank Rate throughout this period remained at 2%. War-time conditions might have been expected to produce a different policy – war brings inflation, and high rates of interest are one way of fighting it – but the Government decided to carry on as before. It was borrowing heavily, and 'dear money' would merely have increased the cost of that borrowing.

After the war, the Labour Government continued with 'cheap money' because it regarded high interest rates as a social evil. People should be able to buy, say, a home of their own without paying an exorbitant price for it. Cheap money was also reckoned to be a useful way of stimulating investment in badly needed new plant and equipment. But by 1951, we once again had a Conservative Government and, partly because of the Korean war boom, we were pushed into a period of rapid inflation and a deteriorating balance of payments. Ministers countered these forces with increased taxes and a higher Bank Rate. Inflation proved more stubborn than anyone had expected, and by the time Mr Wilson's Government took over in 1964 the balance of payments problem, too, had become extremely serious. The new Labour Government refused to devalue the pound, and therefore had no alternative but to keep interest rates comparatively high. By 1970, Bank Rate was up to 8%. It has come down since, but most economists are convinced that the era of really cheap money has gone for good.

## CLEARING BANKS

The handful of banks which are household names – Barclays, Lloyds, Midland, National Westminster. Each day a lot of cheques are paid into their various branches. They are offset against each other in a central 'clearing house', so that banks only have to settle the balance. They do so by drawing a cheque on their own deposits at the Bank of England.

No, it's not a new idea. The 'clearing house' dates back to the eighteenth century.

## CLOSED SHOP

A place of work in which membership of a particular union is a condition of employment. It has always been most prominent in industries where 'craft' unions are in a strong bargaining position, such as printing. When Mr Heath's government began to draw up its Industrial Relations Act, the intention was to ban the closed shop altogether. In the end, however, it introduced something called an 'approved closed shop'. It can be set up where the employer and the union reach voluntary agreement and ask the National Industrial Relations Court for approval. The Court will then decide whether the agreement is in everyone's best interest. In practice, the scheme is likely to have limited application. The Act puts much more emphasis on the establishment of another innovation, the agency shop. This has many of the features of the closed shop: the Act defines it as an agreement between one or more employers and one or more trade unions, in respect of certain workers, that they must belong to one or other of the trade unions in the agreement. But many of the old compulsory features are excluded: it is no longer necessary, for example, for a recruit to belong to a particular union before he is hired – as in printing. The Act as a whole, of course, is an attempt to reform the traditional collective bargaining process.

## COMMON AGRICULTURAL POLICY

A highly controversial scheme devised by the Common Market countries to protect their farmers. Or, as its creators once put it, 'a bargain between German industry and French agriculture'. Germany was the biggest food-importing country; France the biggest surplus-producer. The deal seemed a natural. But the balance of advantages did not work out in Germany's favour, and the German became increasingly critical. The Common Agricultural Policy has been under attack for years, and was held to be one of the main arguments against Britain's entry into the EEC in 1962. Individual countries, including Britain, have long tried to protect their farmers in some way, and the CAP is merely an attempt to provide a common framework, with subsidies made available from a fund to which everyone contributes. But its blatant protectionism is resented in the outside world, and it has plenty of opponents in the EEC itself. The planners have never fully succeeded in coping with one basic fact: Europe produces too much food.


## COMMON MARKET

A commercial arrangement frequently (and erroneously) referred to as 'Europe'. Created in 1958, it aimed at abolishing trade barriers between member countries – and, eventually, at economic integration leading to the long-term goal of political unity. The first aim was achieved within ten years or so, but the others have been much more difficult to accomplish. There is a so-called European parliament, and there is no shortage of European organizations. Indeed, the casual visitor from, say, Japan might be forgiven for concluding that supra-national Europe already exists. But parliaments, councils, committees and other set-ups are a front: they disguise the fact that there is no such thing as a genuine 'European Community'.

The European parliament lacks real power; important decisions are still taken at the national level, as they have always been. When Britain negotiated its own entry in 1971, the Government took great care to stress that no one nation could override another. Britain was keeping her own parliament, courts, and authorities. The English and Scottish legal systems would continue as before. And the 'Community' does not cover defence policies.

Common Market enthusiasts still talk about political unity, but admit that progress is likely to be slow. Even in the commercial field, where the advantages of joining forces appeared most obvious, fact remains far removed from fancy. There is still no European company law, no common currency, no freedom from exchange control. The 'American challenge' has not yet produced the kind of regrouping Jean-Jacques Schreiber, among others, considers so essential. Europe's opinion on Vietnam or Pakistan continues to carry little weight in Washington and Peking and 'European unity' has not been able to prevent outrageous events right on its doorstep, such as the invasion of Czechoslovakia.

History, tradition, and different languages are, of course, the biggest obstacles. But part of the fault must lie with Europe's political leaders. Their visions of Europe have not produced any sense of personal involvement; the young, particularly, regard Brussels as little more than a bureaucratic paradise. Perhaps that will change one day, but it may take an awfully long time.

## COMPANY DOCTOR

An expert sent to save a business, if he can. His title is not an official one: it was bestowed by the financial press because it seemed appropriate. The company doctor is likely to be an accountant, a lawyer, or a management consultant. Occasionally, he is all three. His chief characteristic is an impersonal regard for facts – and the professional ability to assess them. Like any other doctor, he makes his diagnosis, suggests a cure and helps to nurse a company through its difficulties. His desk-side manner is often blunt and abrupt. Company doctors are seldom popular. And few of them are rich. Comfortably off, yes. In the millionaire class, no. As in the medical profession, the real aristocrats are the top surgeons – men like Sir Arnold Weinstock and Jim Slater.

A doctor, someone once said, is a chap who tells you that if you don't cut something out, he will. It's a message lots of businessmen would do well to remember.

## COMPETITIVE SURVEILLANCE

A management catchphrase, coined by a group of Boston consultants. It's long and it scans well: you can quite safely use it at cocktail parties, and the person you are trying to impress won't have the slightest idea what it means. So what does it mean? It means finding out what the other man's doing. It means reading the papers, dissecting his annual report, stripping down and analysing his latest products, and knowing when his top scientist is weary of his job and wants to move. It could also mean, although the Boston Consulting Group doesn't say so, industrial espionage. 'Early intelligence', the Group assures us, 'opens a wide range of tactical options – in pricing, marketing and brinkmanship.' And the pay-off 'can be very great indeed when properly related to the corporate strategy'.

## CONFERENCE
Also known as Convention. An essential feature of the twentieth-century way of life, for several reasons. One is that they keep Britain's many large, old-fashioned, uncomfortable hotels from going out of business. Another is that they satisfy the present-day craving for togetherness. They are a natural extension of committee meetings and annual dinners. They make people feel at home, real, important. Conference man is not simply an individual, plagued by self-doubts. He is part of an important club, a forum which allows a group of people with some common interest to present a united front against the rest. Conferences confer status on those who attend them, and on the bodies who hold them. An organization which can afford to hold a national conference once a year clearly deserves to be taken seriously.

The chief product of conferences are speeches and resolutions. Occasionally, they also produce good ideas, but this is not the purpose of a conference. Newcomers sometimes make the mistake of thinking that they ought to air original thoughts, but they soon learn that this is an unwelcome approach. It challenges the spirit of togetherness, the carefully cultivated impression that everyone is in the same boat, rowing for the common good. Conference man, at his best, is a master of the art of disseminating platitudes. The audience invariably gives him a standing ovation. In contrast, the fellow who tries to be different will usually find himself sitting down amid deafening silence. 'What', one member of the audience will whisper to another, 'is this damn fool talking about?'

# CONFRONTATION

A discussion between opposed parties who sit in separate rooms and communicate through an intermediary. One of the words favoured by newspaper headline writers, because it helps to dramatize particular situations. It's important, if you want to keep a sense of perspective, to familiarize yourself with some of the other headline terms.

CRACKDOWN: any feeble attempt of authority to stand up to the truculence of a minority.

TOUGH BARGAINING: a negotiating session in which management takes a little longer than usual to give in.

BACKLASH: a state of dismay and impotent muttering among groups who feel they are being picked on, but who don't really see what they can do about it.

CRISIS: a flat point in a long-drawn-out, tedious dispute.

TENSE SITUATION: a situation.

GRAVE DEVELOPMENT: a development.

PROSPECTS ARE BLEAK/GRIM/ROSY: prospects are the same as any other day.

VICTORY: any more or less successful exaction of a wage award.

SHOCK: a predictable event likely to be received by the public with apathetic acquiescence. For example: 'Fares Rise Shock', 'Rates Rise Shock'.

LASHES: criticizes.

SLAMS: a milder version of 'Lashes'.

FLAYS: criticizes, with strong rhetorical touches, e.g. 'Clive Jenkins Flays Government'.

OF NATIONWIDE CONCERN: of arguable concern within a couple of miles of Fleet Street.

THREAT TO DEMOCRACY: threat to the press.

LONDON GRINDS TO A HALT: a number of persons trying to reach London to buy and sell shares, go to the cinema or seduce women find that the trains are not running properly and are forced to make other arrangements.

OUCH!: Chancellor takes threepence from everyone.

BONANZA: Chancellor gives threepence to everyone.

# CONGLOMERATE
Take a firm making paper hankies, another importing wine, a third specializing in burglar alarms, and a fourth publishing classics. Put them all together under one corporate roof, and you've got a conglomerate. The late Edward Westropp, one of the best-known financial writers of the fifties, used to have a less fanciful label: a dog's breakfast. The concept behind it is far from new. Many of our great nationalized industries are conglomerates: the Coal Board, for example, is a chemical manufacturer, a landowner, and a farmer as well as a coalminer and distributor. Basically, a conglomerate is a multi-purpose, multi-industry company noted for hodge-podge acquisitions – an enterprise dedicated to proving that oil and water *do* mix.

An essential feature is common financial control and strong central management. From the investor's point of view the idea has considerable appeal: it appears to give him a wide spread of interest. Unfortunately, performance does not always match up to the promise. Sir Fred Catherwood, former Director-General of the National Economic Development Council, is one of the many economists who are highly sceptical about their value. 'There is absolutely no economic case at all', he says, 'for companies merging with others of an entirely dissimilar character. To my mind, a conglomerate is a group where, if one company goes sour, the top management does not know enough about its business to give it advice, and to put it right, and the only option left open is either to sell it off, wind it up, or fire the entire management and hire another lot. The cross-subsidization is entirely uneconomic because it protects operations which should be wound up. What you find in a conglomerate is that one section of the company is making the money, and the board are playing around with the money they're making and dabbling in all kinds of other activities which are making a loss. This is very uneconomic from a national point of view, and from the shareholders' point of view.'

# CONSTANT PRICES
One of the things which annoys economists is that nothing ever seems to stay the same. This is certainly true of prices, and it makes

comparisons with the past not only difficult, but often quite misleading. So for the purpose of theorizing, economists like to assume
that prices have stayed constant. You will sometimes see phrases
like 'at 1936 prices' or 'at 1958 prices'. Don't be fooled; there is, of
course, no such thing. It's simply a splendid way of playing about
with figures, and it's a game all can join. Example: Concorde would
probably have cost £15,000 at 1524 prices!

## CONSUMER DURABLE

A real favourite with economists this; it means, roughly translated,
'goods which last for a period of time', such as furniture, cars,
houses and washing machines. Food and drink are obviously in a
different category, and their link with the word 'consumption' is
more obvious. Economists, though, persist in the notion that furniture and cars, too, are 'consumed' rather than used. They say it's a
more precise term; 'consumed' implies that even durables wear out
and have to be replaced; 'used' has no such implication. They have
a point, but don't apologize if the whole thing strikes you as a bit
odd – you're not alone.

## CONSUMER SOCIETY

A world obsessed with the symbols of material welfare – cars, washing machines, TV sets. A lot of experts on both sides of the Atlantic
hold it responsible for social evils like violence and drug-taking.
Their main target is the advertising industry which, it is said, forces
people to buy more and more things they do not need, and do not
really want.

In Britain, Lord Bath and others talk nostalgically about the
thirties – a time when the rich were rich, and the poor were poor,
and everything was in its rightful place. 'Our motto', his Lordship
says, was 'treat 'em mean, keep 'em keen.' People did not try to
overstep the line. They did not covet luxuries which the Almighty
had reserved for their betters. Hence there was no need for nil
norms, productivity bargaining, freezes, squeezes, courts of inquiry,
and all the other nonsense which nowadays dominates the headlines. In America, students stage demonstrations against the 'mani-
pulation' of the consumer society, and particularly of leisure.

In the Soviet Union, Karl Marx's disciples have taken care not to fall into the same trap. Workers have not been spoiled by things like cars, *dachas,* and refrigerators. Moscow has no traffic problems because prices of the few cars made available every year are fixed at a level which the worker knows he cannot afford. A pair of shoes can cost a week's wages, so there is little left for fripperies. And you will still find several families living in one apartment, just as they used to do in Britain, because the wise men in the Kremlin recognize the need to protect the working class from the influences which are causing so much trouble here. Soviet workers are not compelled to live in degrading luxury.

Contrast this with life in unhappy America and Britain. Sprawling suburbs. Streets choked with cars. A TV set in every home. Fried chicken every day. More and more leisure. Glamorous ads enticing us to travel freely, and cheaply, around the world. If I didn't know better, I'd say it was all a communist plot, an attempt to smother us with prosperity. Some expert, no doubt, will sooner or later say it for me.

## CONSUMPTION

A much misunderstood term because, in economics, it means not only things which are physically consumed – such as food – but also objects and services which are in regular use, such as furniture, and services such as transport and window-cleaning. You can 'consume' a record – or this book – without actually eating it. Chancellors and their advisers are forever trying to measure consumption, because it is so crucial to economic management. They talk about our 'propensity to consume' – meaning the relationship between income and consumer spending. The 'propensity' (a tendency to move in a certain direction) is subject to all kinds of influence; in some circumstances, we tend to save more than in others. The concept was evolved by Keynes and is still very much in use.

## CONTANGO

One of the Stock Exchange's more exotic terms, meaning that you can 'carry' a speculation over into the next account if dealers are willing. The Stock Exchange divides its year into 'accounts' which normally last two weeks, although there are a few which last three. If you buy and sell a share within the same account, you don't pay stamp duty and are normally charged less commission. Speculators frequently whip in and out of a share if they have reason to expect news which will dramatically affect the price. It sometimes pays off, and sometimes doesn't. It's amazing how many people will back wild and absurd rumours. But there are occasions when the information is right, but the timing wrong. This is where the contango comes in. If you've bought the shares for the account, and you show a loss, you may be able to arrange to transfer the deal to the next account – for a fee. But watch your step: a lot depends on your broker and on the popularity of the shares concerned. If there is an active market in them it's a lot easier to contango than if the market is a narrow one. Dealers have no more enthusiasm for unpleasant surprises than the rest of us.

## CONVERTIBILITY
Freedom to exchange one nation's currency for another. If you travel from Britain to the United States or France you can convert your pounds into dollars or francs at the airport, or any bank. More than thirty countries have made their paper money freely convertible in this way. Many, though, apply some form of restriction on transfers of capital, and even on the total sum exchanged by travellers on each trip. And some carry their restrictions so far that, in effect, their currency is not convertible at all. They include the iron curtain countries and China, and poor nations who dare not risk having their citizens swap local money for so-called 'hard currency' (see page 100).

The term 'convertibility' at one time meant convertible into gold. This is now comparatively rare. Even the United States, the richest country in the world, had to suspend convertibility when too many people tried their hand at it in the late sixties and early seventies.

## COOLING OFF PERIOD
A device, borrowed from America, for getting union members back to work during an industrial dispute. The British Government first made use of it during the railway go-slow in 1972. Union members were ordered not to take part in any strike or any industrial action

short of a strike during a fourteen-day period. Union leaders were instructed to take all reasonable steps to ensure this was followed.

The device is politically popular, but is of doubtful industrial value, mainly because there is no guarantee whatever that it will solve a labour dispute. A cooling-off period, if fully effective, only suspends action for up to sixty days. Unless the unions actually 'cool off', industrial action can be restarted – as has happened in America – when the period expires.

## CORPORATION TAX
A straight percentage levy on profits of all companies, in place of income and profits tax. Introduced by the Labour Government of 1964–70, it was designed to end the practice of taxing companies and individuals in the same way. This, it was explained, would bring us 'into line with reality' and conform with 'general practice throughout the world'.

Less emphasis was put on two other factors. One, that it would make it easier to penalize companies who chose to pay out dividends to shareholders rather than use the money for purposes which Labour considered more useful, such as buying new machinery. Two, the balance of payments could be helped by inserting clauses which increased taxation on income arising from overseas investment; the idea was to encourage firms to invest their money at home. Considering the urgent need for modernization (inadequate capital investment has been one of Britain's handicaps since the Second World War) the Labour Government's motives were by no means wrong. Many businessmen, nevertheless, felt compelled to protest. The Tories, under Mr Heath, have made some changes (one move has been to end the bias against distributed profits) but corporation tax as such is here to stay.

## COST-BENEFIT ANALYSIS
A method increasingly used by governments to determine the effectiveness of public spending, in relation to costs, in meeting stated objectives. It tries to put a monetary value on services which, by their nature, have no market in which their value could otherwise be tested. A frequently cited example is motorways: attempts

55

are nowadays made to estimate the 'return' which we, the public, get from them and compare it with alternative uses of government funds. There are, of course, considerable snags in this type of calculation and often cost-benefit analysis tends to be of little more than academic interest. Take defence: how do you calculate the benefit we derive from a nuclear submarine, or a jet fighter, or the atom bomb? They may prevent a war, but no accountant likes to put a price on something that hasn't happened, and may never happen. Still, cost-benefit analysis is an advance on the old hit-and-miss methods. Its value shouldn't be overrated, but with government spending nowadays such a huge operation it helps to have at least *some* financial yardstick.

## COST-CUTTING

Popular panic reaction to a fall in profits. Practised with special vigour when the economy is stagnant. Frequently starts with the managing director touring the office at night, snapping off light switches and turning the heater down two degrees. Sometimes a healthy thing, because companies do get careless in their supervision of costs when business is booming. But also potentially dangerous because a sudden fury of indiscriminate cost slashing can destroy the confidence of staff and customers. Key employees may decide to seek safer jobs. Customers and suppliers may stop ordering and suppliers may refuse to give credit. Cost-cutting, moreover, usually hits sections which seem dispensable, but in reality are not. Advertising, research, training programmes – these tend to be among the first victims. A much more sensible policy is to keep an eye on costs all the year round, and to avoid potentially embarrassing commitments. But if you do happen to run into a madman with an axe, an effective counter-ploy is to send him memos listing all the savings you have made by not doing something.

The potential is truly staggering. Think of the money a company like ICI could save by not building new factories. Or the economies publishers could achieve by not producing any books. The ploy also works for governments. Chancellors could announce, on Budget day, that they have saved us, say, £500 million by not putting up taxes. And the Foreign Secretary could chip in with the cheering news that he's saved the nation £4,000 million by not declaring war on the Soviet Union. This could be repeated, with variations, whenever the opinion polls indicate a downturn in ministerial popularity.

## COST OF LIVING INDEX

An official attempt, first started in 1914, to measure price changes throughout the whole field of goods and services over which household expenditure is distributed. Strictly speaking, it is not a cost of living index at all but a price index. It does not measure changes in the kinds and amounts of goods and services people buy, or in the total amount spent in order to live. Nor does it measure differences in living costs between different localities. Income tax, national insurance contributions, subscriptions to trade unions, doctors' fees and many other items are excluded. The index covers the following main groups of items: food, alcoholic drink, tobacco, housing, fuel and light, durable household goods, clothing and footwear, transport and vehicles, miscellaneous goods, services. Each group consists of a number of separate sections: altogether prices are regularly collected by government officials for nearly 350 separate commodities and services. Some of these, of course, are much more important than others; for example, most households spend much more on bread than on soap. Each percentage change, therefore, is 'weighted' to represent its relative importance in the household budget.

A period of four to five weeks is usually needed to do all the homework. The all-items figure for any month, therefore, usually becomes available in the third week of the following month. It is announced in a brief communiqué to the press, and is usually pounced upon by politicians – who love to use it as ammunition against their opponents – and trade union officials, who see any increase as a powerful prop for their wage claims.

## CRAWLING PEG

Basically, a way of making small and, if necessary, frequent changes, either up or down, in exchange rates. The international monetary system set up after the Second World War provided for the price

57

of each currency to be fixed at a certain level – the pivot being the US dollar. This was supposed to be adjustable whenever it became obvious that changing circumstances had made a price unrealistic. In practice, countries proved increasingly reluctant to adjust: maintaining a fixed rate became a matter of national pride. The crawling peg theory was advocated as a means of achieving the necessary adjustment with the minimum of fuss. A major change might cause a public outcry; a crawl would go almost unnoticed. (See FIXED PARITIES and FLOATING.)

## CREDIT CARD
A device to make you spend more. Money, in the old-fashioned sense of coins and notes, is out of date. It certainly is no longer a status symbol: Americans who insist on settling bills in cash are increasingly regarded with suspicion. They look like have-nots who cannot be trusted with charge accounts and credit cards. One does not need a wallet full of banknotes these days to travel around the US. Indeed, it is advisable – because it is safer – to leave it at home. Stores, hotels, supermarkets, petrol stations, car hire firms, restaurants, airlines, and many others have all got away from paper money. Even ambulance services and mortuaries take credit cards, and there's a sign outside a San Francisco Church which proclaims that your card is good for the collection plate. If it were not for the tiresome necessity of tipping doormen and cab-drivers, America would be closer still to fulfilment of the ultimate dream: a cashless society.

In Britain we have been somewhat slower to change our ways, but no one would dispute that things are not what they were. The banks, which used to be so stuffy, have joined the credit card boom with surprising enthusiasm. There are bankers who believe that, by the end of the century, we may be able to dispense with coins and banknotes altogether. This may strike you as far-fetched, but if you look at the change in attitudes – and customs – over the past thirty years it seems by no means impossible that cash will eventually become obsolete. It is already feasible, if you are so minded, to live without ever touching a single pound note. The cheque has long ceased to be a novelty, even among the working class, and the stigma once attached to borrowing has gone for good. Anyone who suggests, today, that hire-purchase is immoral would be dismissed as a crank. The wage packet still exists, but millions now have their earnings paid directly into a bank. Luncheon vouchers have been popular for years, and expense account living merely requires a signature. Travellers' cheques are as widely used as season tickets and credit cards. In short, one can get by on book-keeping transactions. There is no doubt that we shall travel further along this road. The process will be hastened by inflation, as it has been already. As money buys less and less, the conventional coinage and currency will seem more and more inappropriate. For banks and traders, handling currency is expensive, time consuming and unhygienic. The printing of notes and the manufacture of coins involves considerable cost. So does the elaborate business of moving it around the country, with the constant necessity of counting it, packing it, and protecting it. Theoretically, there is no need for any of this. All that matters is that people should be ready and willing to accept whatever form of payment is in fashion. It's not the money as such that counts, but what it will buy.

## CRITICAL PATH ANALYSIS
An impressive way of saying that you are going to look at something in detail. The idea is to (a) break it down into component parts and (b) examine each part both in isolation and in its relationship to the other parts. Hopefully, this will show how a given project can be finished in the best possible way in the quickest possible time. For example, if you are building a factory a critical path analysis will reveal that you should concrete the floor before the machinery is delivered, but after you've laid the drains! Anyone who has dealt with the building industry will know that this principle is not as widely accepted as it should be.

## CUM DIVIDEND
Stock market term meaning 'with dividend'. An investor who buys 'cum' is entitled to the current dividend payment. The shares 'go ex' on a certain specified day, and it's always a good idea to check the position with your stockbroker. The words 'cum' and 'ex' are

also used in connection with scrip and rights issues; 'cum all' means 'with all advantages'.

## CUSTOMS AND EXCISE

Taxes such as tobacco duty, beer, wines and spirit duty, and purchase tax. They are indirect taxes – that is, collected through importers, manufacturers, distributors and other intermediaries – and are a way of bringing everyone into the tax net. Political parties have always argued about this very point: left-wingers argue, with justice, that it's the easiest tax for the wealthy man and the worst for the poor. Customs duty was in existence long before the Excise, or New Impost, was introduced for the first time in Britain during the Civil War, in 1643. It was imported from the continent, and opened the way for an extraordinary range of devices, including a hearth tax and a window tax. The puritans invented it, but the Excise stayed on when the monarchy was restored in 1660 – and, of course, remains with us today.

One of its many advantages, from the government's point of view, is that few people realize just how much they hand over in this indirect way. Could you say, without looking up Customs and Excise Tables, how much duty you are paying on a bottle of Scotch? Or even on a packet of cigarettes? Another is that it allows ministers to make moral judgments: by varying the rate of duty, they can put up the cost of anything they consider bad for us.

## DATA

Fancy substitute – it comes from the Latin *datum* – for the more familiar word 'facts'. I don't know who first decided that it sounded more imposing, but it has certainly caught on in a most remarkable way. Advertising and marketing men are particularly fond of it, you should certainly know the difference between hard data and soft data: the one means numerical measurements and the other 'insights which are not expressible in numerical terms', such as the 'personality' of a newspaper.

## DEBENTURES

Stocks issued by a company in return for long-term loans. They are a debt on the company and, as with a mortgage, are normally secured on part or all of the fixed assets such as property, plant and machinery. Debentures are entitled to a fixed rate of interest, which has to be paid whether the company makes enough profits or not. If it doesn't have the funds, debenture holders can foreclose, put in a receiver, or take other action to protect their interests. In short, they are the safest form of stock on the market. Some may be redeemed (repaid) at a specific date or over a stated number of years, and others may be irredeemable, meaning that the capital is not repaid unless and until the company goes out of business. Debentures are popular with investors who want to combine safety with a reasonable rate of income. But they don't share in profits and, therefore, are no safeguard against inflation. The market price, moreover, depends to some extent on the general level of interest prevailing at any given time. So even with debentures there is no absolute *guarantee* that the value of your investment will always stay exactly the same.

## DEBTOR

A person who owes money to another. The stigma once attached to it has long disappeared; nowadays everyone runs up debts at one time or another. Personally I would much rather be a debtor than a creditor, especially at times of rapid inflation. Say you borrow £10,000 and undertake to pay it back in five years' time. If you invest it wisely, the chances are that the value of your holding, at the end of that period, will show an increase which will not only make up for the interest you have paid on the loan, but will also give you a useful capital gain. Your repayment will be exactly £10,000, but in terms of purchasing power that sum will be worth a lot less than it was five years' earlier. In short, you are repaying in devalued currency. During that five years, moreover, the creditor has a vested interest in your financial health. A bank manager who has helped to set you up in business will want to protect his loan: the chances are that, if you run into temporary financial difficulty, he will give you further assistance rather than risk losing the money altogether. A creditor (i.e. a person to whom money is owed) is in a strong legal position, and in theory can recover his loan at any given time. In practice, though, he tends to be much more at the mercy of events than is generally acknowledged. (See BAD DEBTS.)

## DEED OF COVENANT

Basically an agreement under which one person undertakes to pay a fixed sum to another for a certain period of time. Underlying the deed of covenant is one aim: to transfer taxable income from one to the other. The Inland Revenue, not surprisingly, has always treated such deeds with a great deal of hostility, and successive Finance Acts have gradually narrowed the scope. The most famous clash took place more than forty years ago. and involved the Duke of Westminster. The Duke's legal advisers felt it would be smart to execute numerous deeds of covenant for the benefit of employees and others. Both the commissioners before whom the case was first heard and a distinguished revenue judge took the view that the covenanted payments were a disguised form of remuneration and therefore not eligible in relief of the Duke's tax. The Court of Appeal and the House of Lords took the opposite view. The end result was that, although the Duke got away with it, legislation was later passed to end arrangements of this kind. Today many people make deeds of covenant in favour of children, or of charity, but it pays to consult a tax expert before taking any such step.

## DE-ESCALATE

Reduce. A favourite with trade union leaders and others. A top official, not long ago, said he would 'do his best to stop the escalation of official action'.

He wouldn't dream of talking like that to his wife or friends, but somehow it seems to be assumed that plain English won't do on these occasions. A *Financial Times* reader pointed out, cheekily, that the word 'de-escalate' means 'the incorporation of mission constraints on a reducing basis, independent of functional principles'. Well, yes, certainly. But how about a meaningful de-escalation of jargon, or, putting it another way, a spot of dejargonization?

## DENIAL

Firm insistence that a rumour is incorrect. Seldom accepted at its face value. It's taken for granted that every businessman, or economist, or politician tells lies from time to time. Not only taken for granted, but excused on the grounds that, if everyone went around telling the truth on each and every occasion, society as we know it would be in mortal danger. Journalists have long worked on the premise that when a man says one thing, he usually means exactly the opposite.

In the United States, politicians aspiring to the White House invariably announce that they are not candidates, which means that they most certainly are. In the business world, you can usually tell that a deal is on the point of being clinched by the vigour of the denials that anything is going on at all. When the Labour Government decided to devalue the pound in 1967, it went on denying for a whole week after the decision had been taken that anything so awful had even been discussed. And there have been countless occasions, during the years of merger mania, when take-over deals have been firmly denied right up to a minute before the public announcement of the actual details. There are, alas, a few people who do not, as yet, appear to know about the new convention. They continue to issue denials in the old-fashioned expectation that everyone will accept them as the last word. The denials confuse those who have come to regard them as the most reliable form of confirmation, and it may be helpful to provide a brief guideline:

(1) If you want people to think that you didn't do it, issue a public statement saying that you did. Then no one will believe you.

(2) If you want to take credit for something that has gone well, deny that you have had anything to do with it. Then journalists will automatically assume that you are merely being modest.

(3) If you don't want people to know about a deal that's still in the pipeline, do not on any account issue a denial. Say 'sure, and I'm taking over ICI and Courtaulds as well'. The City will take that as a clear sign that you're not involved in negotiations of any kind.

(4) If you want to leak some piece of good news, tell it to a friend in 'strict confidence', and sit by your telephone waiting for the inevitable call from the journalist. Pretend to be surprised and disconcerted, and issue a vague denial. He will then realize that he's got a scoop, and the news will be splashed on page one. If

63

you merely make a public announcement, it will be tucked away at the bottom of page 14.

There are various well-established phrases to use on all these occasions, and you ought to know at least a few of them.

'This is absolutely untrue' means 'yes, it's true, but you don't expect me to say so, do you?' A variation of this is 'I don't know what you are talking about'. It means he hopes you, the questioner, don't know what you're talking about. 'This is absurd' means 'he is on to something there'. And 'yes, we are negotiating with ICI' means 'no, we're not, but we would like to'.

## DEVALUATION

Reducing the value of a country's currency in terms of foreign currencies.

In 1967, Britain devalued by 14·3% – meaning that, henceforth, the pound would buy that much less in terms of dollars. Devaluation makes it cheaper for foreigners to buy our products, and eventually leads to bigger exports. But it also means that we have to pay more for everything we buy abroad, including food. A country which frequently devalues, moreover, finds that foreign traders lose confidence in its paper money. They exchange it for something else – gold, or raw materials – as quickly as they can. No one wants to be stuck with paper which can lose its value overnight.

Devaluation also has a more indirect effect on confidence at home: the higher cost of imports after 1967, and the publicity given to the 'downfall' of the pound, are widely believed to have triggered off the severe bout of inflation which followed. This is why the Bank of England and others strongly disapprove of devaluation. Many economists do not agree. They argue that, once it is clear that a country's currency is no longer worth the price asked for it, it's best to devalue at once rather than go through the long and tiresome business of defending the existing exchange rate. They say that Mr Wilson – and later General de Gaulle – made the mistake of turning a fixed exchange rate into a national prestige symbol. 'The pound', Mr Wilson announced in 1964, 'is in danger.' By implication, the country was in danger too. We were fighting for survival. This, economists maintain, is arrant nonsense. A nation's survival does not depend on its ability to maintain a certain rate against the dollar, and to invoke Dunkirk in such situation is bogus patriotism.

## DIMINISHING RETURNS (LAW OF)
A phrase you simply must know if you want to show that you understand economics. The law is relatively simple: at a certain point it does not pay to add to the effort to improve, say, a piece of land. Additional outlay does not correspondingly increase the return. Carried far enough, it will reduce it. The law also applies to other activities, notably the raising of taxes. A government cannot tax, say, tobacco or drinks *ad infinitum*. Sooner or later it reaches the point where another increase produces such a sharp fall in sales that, on balance, the extra tax produces very little extra revenue or actually leads to a drop in the overall income.

## DISCOUNT HOUSES
Highly specialized financial institutions which make short-term loans to the Government by buying Treasury bills (*see* page 187) and bonds. They also lend to private industry by holding commercial bills of exchange, but this is a much less important function than it used to be in the nineteenth century, when the discount market was a major source of finance for industry and trade. The houses get most of their money from the commercial banks, and many people argue that they have outlived their purpose. But they are still there – a hangover from the past, making their profits by borrowing at a lower rate of interest than their lending rate, and showing a remarkable degree of resilience.

## DISCOUNTING NEWS
Newcomers to investment are sometimes surprised to find that the stock market's reaction to good news is the opposite of what they had expected: a higher dividend may actually be followed by a decline in price. This is because the market has already 'discounted' the news, meaning that it has correctly anticipated what the company concerned will do. Any well-known growth stock is closely followed

by a lot of people, and professionals usually have a fairly good idea what to expect. It doesn't always happen, of course, and the discounting process also works in the case of bad news. A dividend cut may have been allowed for several weeks in advance (nervous people will have sold their stock) and the actual announcement will be greeted with relief that the setback has not proved any bigger. With the worst known, new buyers may well be attracted by the possibility that, next year, the former rate will be restored. Company boards often regard it as a matter of pride to make good a dividend cut at the earliest opportunity.

Discounting, of course, also happens in the market as a whole. The Stock Exchange usually runs ahead of the economy, or individual industries, and a pick-up in profits may well be allowed for months ahead of the published confirmation.

## DIVERSIFICATION

Spreading your risk by making several products, investing in different shares, or moving into new fields through the acquisition of other companies.

The stock market is understandably cautious about 'one product firms' because conditions can so easily turn against them. The John Bloom crash, some years ago, is a frequently quoted example. Bloom started with a good idea. It was not particularly original or complicated. But he pushed forward with supreme self-confidence and energetic enthusiasm, it caught on brilliantly. The washing machine giants were selling their products through the shops, handing retailers a large profit margin. Bloom eliminated the retailer, and went all out for big sales. He used every gimmick in the book, and a few new ones, to build up the kind of volume he wanted. But to become another Wolfson, Clore or Fraser you need more than a single idea. You can spot a gap in big industry's armour and exploit it vigorously. But as soon as you've proved yourself you must look around for fresh fields to conquer. Bloom realized the dangers of sticking to the washing machine business alone once the slumbering giants had been awakened. He desperately tried to repeat his success in other fields. But he was impatient, and he revelled in publicity. When the crash came he was in Bulgaria, of all places, trying to fix up a contract for package tours. It never got off the ground.

Many well-known, highly respectable companies have also found that successful diversification is easier said than done. Distillers, world-famous for its brands of whisky and gin, launched out into the industrial field many years ago and built up a separate chemicals division. Not long ago, however, the directors glady sold the major part of the group's chemical interests to British Petroleum – and announced that they planned to plough the money back into their traditional liquor business. Guinness has built up extensive interests in the confectionery business, through the acquisition of various companies, but is still very much on the 'one product' hook. British American Tobacco acquired the Yardley cosmetics firm in 1967, and also the Toni-bell ice-cream business. Imperial Tobacco, worried by the declining scope for its principal product, went into potato crisps, teaching machines, and electronic equipment. All would, I am sure, readily admit that diversification is full of pitfalls.

## DOLLAR IMPERIALISM

Another way of saying 'we take your cash, but we don't like it'. The phrase is a firm favourite with left-wing students and others who claim that America has tried to build an empire with money. Hitting at US investment has long been fashionable all over the world; the late General de Gaulle was simply one of the more prominent attackers. But dollar imperialism is also reckoned to work through foreign aid. America, it's said, uses aid to maintain a position of influence and control around the world. Washington takes little trouble to deny it: economic assistance is felt to be a useful method of sustaining countries which might otherwise pass into the communist bloc. In short, to the White House dollar imperialism is a virtue; to its critics, it's a vice. There are times when Congress, reflecting the mood of a large segment of the American public, finds it all too much and votes to reduce foreign aid – or even to eliminate it altogether. This happened in 1971, and is primarily an expression of resentment against 'ungrateful allies'. Aid, a senator declared, 'has for too long been regarded as a bottomless pit for free-loading nations who victimize Uncle Sucker'.

Americans have always had a great need for affection and approval. They expect gratitude and love: they get criticism and hostility. It is a reaction with which older nations, like Britain, are more than familiar. No one ever really loves a lender. His generosity is welcomed at first, but then gives way to suspicion and resentment. People don't like to be dependent on someone else. And they certainly don't want constant reminders that they have had to accept charity. Some of the strongest attacks on dollar imperialism have come from countries who would be far worse off without it. It's a phenomenon, of course, which is familiar to individuals as well as governments: the quickest way to lose a friend is to help him get started in business, or to tide him over a bad patch.

## DOLLAR PREMIUM

Anyone buying dollar stocks from London has to use special 'investment dollars'. As there is a limited supply the investor has to pay a premium for them. This can amount to 30% or more, and therefore represents a considerable handicap to investing on Wall Street.

## DOW-JONES

Shorthand for the Dow-Jones index, Wall Street's best-known barometer. It is named after Charles H. Dow, the first editor of *The Wall Street Journal*, who started to compile daily averages of stock prices in 1897. Dow Jones now consists of four averages: one for 30 industrials, one for 20 rails, one for 15 utilities, and a 65-stock composite of these three groups. They are calculated and announced every half an hour during the New York Exchange trading day.

The Dow Theory is based on the view that an index of stocks and shares reflects all that is generally known about the outlook for business in general, and expresses all the hopes and fears about the prospects for the individual companies whose shares make up the index. Movements of Dow's indices were analysed and it was found that certain patterns tended to repeat themselves, so that it was possible to predict future index movements with some degree of success. Some modern analysts are sceptical about the value of this approach, and it is certainly possible to make out a case against some of the claims made by Dow enthusiasts. But the indices themselves have acquired such a wide following, and have such an important psychological impact, that they are unquestionably a major factor on Wall Street.

In Britain, *The Financial Times* provides the nearest thing to Dow Jones. The FT Industrial Ordinary Index consists of 30 shares, all of them active stocks in the country's leading industrial companies. It was started in 1935; its lowest point since then was in 1940, and its highest in 1972. There are also FT indices for government stocks, general fixed interest securities, and gold mines.

## DUMPING

A term used in international trade to describe the unloading of a particular product in another country at a low price. A company in, say, Britain may find its own market so saturated that it prefers to 'dump' a sizeable part of its output in the United States or in Europe at a low profit rather than at none at all. Or it may have such a monopoly position at home that it can get away with restricting home sales, and charging a high price, and 'dumping' the rest abroad at a price which the local producer simply cannot afford to match. There are all kinds of international agreements to prevent this sort of thing, and in practice deliberate large-scale dumping is by no means easy. It usually needs the cooperation – or, at least, compliance, of one's own government, and everyone involved knows there is always a risk of retaliation. Communist countries are clearly well placed to go in for dumping, but since most of their trade with the West is regulated by quotas they tend not to get away with it. With others, the dividing line between dumping and stiff competition may be rather thin – and one often hears cries of 'unfair, unfair' when all that's really happening is that a foreign competitor is more efficient than the local firm.

## ECONOMIC CRISIS

Every Englishman's favourite phrase. No one does a crisis as well as we do. The Americans may be better at riots, and the Danes superior at pornography, but when it comes to an economic crisis Britain is well out in front.

So, of course, we should be. Who, after all, has more experience? We have had an economic crisis for as long as anyone can remember; it is a British institution. The language of crisis is ours: 'export or die', the 'trade gap', and the 'Dunkirk spirit' are all British inventions. And no one has spent as much time pulling up socks, tightening belts, rolling up sleeves, and putting backs to the wall. Without the British economic crisis, no one would ever have heard of the Gnomes of Zürich, central bankers, and the International Monetary Fund. It would never have occurred to anyone that nations must export or die. Trade gaps and balance of payments would have remained undiscovered. No wonder foreign TV crews and newspapermen flock here to observe what has become known, throughout the world, as 'the English sickness'. Everyone wants to know how we do it, and how we manage to keep it up. From a TV producer's point of view, of course, an economic crisis tends to produce certain technical difficulties. It's easy enough to assemble a few experts in the studio, and let them ramble on for an hour or so. But if you send a crew out on location, you have to find something they can point their cameras at. And that leaves out things like a balance of payments deficit. In Britain, happily, this tends to be less of a problem than in other countries. There is a routine schedule, used countless times, which can be completed in three days, and which looks something like this:

First day. Morning at Buckingham Palace, to film the Changing of the Guard. This establishes that Britain is still obsessed by tradition, and totally out of touch with the twentieth century. Nice shots of horses, soldiers, etc. Afternoon in factory on outskirts of London, to film British workers drinking tea. This shows that the British are lazy, and explains why Britain has fallen behind in the rat race.

Second day. Morning in Hyde Park, filming trade union demonstration. This shows that when they are not drinking tea, English workers are marching up and down, shouting slogans and singing the 'Red Flag'. Excellent shots of Pakistanis and West Indians marching by their side; this shows that immigrants can't help catching the English disease. Afternoon in hired studio, filming interview with politician or economist who will confirm that the British economic crisis is still going strong—that, indeed, Britain is down and out, finished. This establishes the crew's impartiality.

**Third day.** Morning in Carnaby Street to film British decadence. Wonderful shots of girls in hot pants. This establishes that the British do not care about their economic problems – that they are only interested in having fun. Afternoon in Soho taking shots of queues outside strip clubs for extra emphasis.

The schedule, as you can see, allows a crew to collect enough material for an hour's in-depth study of a derelict empire. It is not necessary, as a rule, to send your commentator along as well, because he can get most of his opinions from the British press. There will, inevitably, be people who seek to spoil everything by claiming that, for a relatively small country, we don't do at all badly. There may even be some who argue that Britain is a more pleasant country to live in than economically successful societies like the United States and Japan. The younger generation, particularly, seems to be prone to this kind of dangerous thinking. Fortunately, our own press can be relied upon to attack such foolish notions. Britain without a crisis is nothing at all: sackcloth and ashes are our national dress and misery – pretended or otherwise – our most valued tradition.

## ECONOMIC MAN
A mythical creature, used as a convenient abstraction in discussing economic affairs. Economists, as a rule, base their theories chiefly on how rational people might behave in a certain situation on the basis of certain assumptions. The main assumption is that Economic Man has an overwhelming urge to maximize his wealth with the minimum of sacrifice. This is enshrined in a hundred textbooks: if X happens, Y is supposed to follow.

The trouble is that comparatively few people read the textbooks. They are guided by instinct rather than knowledge. And instinct frequently makes them go in for behaviour which, to the academic, seems bewilderingly irrational. This might not matter so much if conditions were still the same as twenty or thirty years ago. The textbooks suggest plenty of ways in which people can be brought to heel. But conditions are not the same. Economists all over the world admit that they have not yet learned to cope with the combined force of affluence, bloody-mindedness, and trade union power. Economic Man frequently acts in a way which appears to run counter to his best interests: he prefers leisure to making more money, brings his employers (and himself) to ruin by indulging in pointless strikes, and panics when commonsense requires that he should be calm. Younger Economic Man also tends to react differently from older Economic Man. He is, for example, less easily shaken by the threat of unemployment. It's not just that greatly improved unemployment benefits have taken away some of the sting. A more potent influence is, quite simply, that workers who have not experienced conditions like those of the thirties are less easily frightened.

## ECONOMIES OF SCALE
The benefits of size. A supermarket chain which can buy in bulk gets economies of scale which are denied to the small shopkeeper. A manufacturer operating in, say, the motor industry can reduce the cost of each new car through long runs of ouput or standardized parts. This has been the reasoning behind the merger boom of recent years: larger units, it has been argued, are more able to take on foreign competition than small ones. There is, clearly, a great deal to be said for this kind of thinking. The economies of scale are not a pipe-dream. But experience suggests that they often take a good deal longer to achieve than directors would have investors believe at the time of the merger. And size can produce all kinds of problems. Size alone is certainly no guarantee of greater efficiency. The advantages of scale, if they are not to be outweighed by the disadvantages, are not automatic, but have to be worked for in a climate of sustained economic expansion. They can only be gained if plants

are working at, or near, full capacity. There's also the question of market power; in many cases, it is against the interest of consumers – which means you and I – to have any one firm gain too much of a hold on any particular trade or industry.

## EFFICIENCY

Today's watchword – it's what the other fellow doesn't have enough of. Politicians find it a useful peg for non-committal speeches, and company chairmen like to include it in their annual statement on the principle that if you talk about it loud enough no one will suspect *you* of shortcomings. No businessman, of course, admits to being inefficient – and why should he? As long as you are making money, it's all a matter of opinion. It's easy to hit up new profit peaks each year by employing more and more capital (plenty of firms get a reputation for efficiency that way) and it isn't hard to convince yourself that, if your earnings are not all they should be, it is purely because you have a decent sense of priority. Staff and customers come before profit: you are a modern manager.

Prosperous trading conditions do not make for maximum efficiency. When business is booming, all sorts of things go unnoticed. Parkinson's law tends to work overtime: every petty section head can quietly add one or two people to the staff. New ventures are looked at less critically and old machinery is kept working flat out. No one wants to risk disruption when order books stretch way ahead. A different attitude tends to develop when business slackens and profit margins come under pressure; suddenly, boards start to ask themselves questions. There's nothing like a good, old-fashioned setback to make company directors doubt their own genius.

## ENDOWMENT

Endow is another word for bequeath or 'give to', and is associated mainly with insurance policies. Basically it means that, by paying a certain sum, the holder of the policy becomes entitled to a fixed amount at a stated date. 'With profit' endowment policies (entitling the holder to bonus payments) have become the most popular form of life insurance in Britain. People who borrow from a building society often use it as a way of repaying a mortgage. By taking out a

C*

policy which matures in, say, twenty-five years a borrower can be sure that his family will be protected if he should die. He also gets income tax relief on the premiums. Other forms of special endowment include educational policies; the insurance company undertakes to pay educational bills from an agreed age over an agreed period.

## ENTREPRENEUR

One who undertakes an enterprise; an individual who owns the business and takes the risk. You will come across the word in economic textbooks, but just about the only people who use it nowadays are economists and financial writers. Even in France, an entrepreneur is more commonly referred to as *le businessman*. The entrepreneurial function is held to be a central concept in economics, and many theories are built on it. Some still hold water, but others have been out-dated by drastic changes in industrial structure – the managers who now run the biggest companies are not entrepreneurs in the original sense.

## EQUITY

The popular name for ordinary shares. They are the risk capital, taking the benefits if things go well, and shouldering all or the bulk of the loss if they go badly. Most companies have loan capital, preference shares or some other stock which has prior claim on both earnings and assets. Interest and dividends on these has to be paid out of the year's profits before anything is made available for distribution to equity holders. If the company should go bust, equity holders are last in the queue. Because of this, they are generally more subject to price fluctuations than debentures or preference shares. Their main attraction is that, unlike the others, they share in the company's prosperity. They also have a vote, which means they are the bosses. Well, that's the theory anyway. In practice, things tend to be a bit more complicated.

Few companies pay out all their surplus in the form of dividends. A Board of Directors may, for example, decide that it needs a big part of the surplus to finance expansion or modernization. The dividend will, in that case, be kept at the same level even though the company may have had an excellent year. The equity holder ultimately benefits, because the company is – or should be – enhancing its earnings power and adding to the assets backing for the shares. But it could mean a temporary setback in the share price.

As an owner, the equity holder is free to complain. But it is by no means easy to take on the board of one of today's big corporations – unless, perhaps, you have 15% or 20% of the equity. Just about the only time when your vote really counts is during a take-over battle, when equity holders tend to be wooed by both sides with considerable ardour. (See ANNUAL GENERAL MEETING.)

## ERGONOMICS
A word so new you won't find it in *The Concise Oxford Dictionary*. It means the scientific study of ordinary people in work situations, and has become highly fashionable with the advent of 'behavioural science'. It is, of course, a marked improvement on the days when twelve-year-old children were sent down a mine, regardless of human consequences. Ergonomics, and/or behavioural science, tries to apply modern methods to the design of processes and machines, to the lay-out of work places, to methods of work, and to 'job satisfaction', in order to get greater efficiency of both men and machines. In short, it acknowledges the importance of people in the money-making process. The trouble is that workers often behave in an illogical contradictory way. Bloody-mindedness, for example, constantly gets in the way of theories. One result is that, as with economics, scientists often give up the struggle and stick to theorizing or writing papers for examiners and other practitioners in the field. (See also: IN-PLANT FEEDING STATION and ECONOMIC MAN.)

## ERNIE
Affectionate name for the electronic machines which pick the premium bond prize winners. They have thousands of visitors each year – apart from the pen pals who send them cans of oil, boxes of chocolates and cigars. Premium Bonds were launched in 1956, and continue to enjoy great popularity. There are more than twenty million holders of bonds in Britain. The main reason for their success, unquestionably, is that they are a gamble, and a very special kind of gamble at that. Instead of interest, you have a regular chance

to win a cash prize. And there's no risk of losing. Bonds are available at any post office, in units of £2, and they are entered for the draw after they have been held three clear months. Each month nearly 60,000 prizes are distributed, ranging in value from £25 to £50,000.

Critics say the odds against winning a really big prize are too great, and that unless you are exceptionally lucky the amount of money you're likely to win, even if you have a full allocation of bonds, won't equal the annual rate of interest you could earn elsewhere. But for most bondholders this is really beside the point. The sophisticated argument about interest rate differentials leaves them cold: it's the thrill that counts.

## EURO-BOND MARKET

Set up in 1963, it has established as the most versatile (and volatile) capital market in Europe. Like the Euro-dollar (see below), it owes its existence largely to US government restrictions designed to help the balance of payments. US firms tried to raise money in Europe instead, and the Euro-bond made its appearance. The market is chiefly meant for businessmen who want to borrow for periods of ten years or more, and is used by many other people besides the Americans. Its growth was helped by the narrowness of continental money markets, and today it overshadows all national centres – accommodating a wider range of borrowers than any other. Investors, too, find advantages in buying Euro-bonds and there is now a Euro-dollar equity – suitable for American companies wishing to raise funds overseas.

At first, Euro-bonds were nearly always issued in Euro-dollars. This meant that any investor in any European country who had Euro-dollars could buy the issue. More recently, Euro-bonds have also been issued in other European currencies who have established their strength and general acceptability – notably the German mark.

## EURO-DOLLARS

A controversial 'currency' which did not really make an impact until the mid-fifties, but then had a spectacular career. They are, basically, dollars accumulated in Europe from large American overseas net lending and spending. The dollars found their way into Europe's commercial banks, and eventually a market was established in them. The Euro-dollar market was given a big boost in 1968, when President Johnson put controls on further dollar outflows for investment in Europe. American firms tried to find dollars anywhere they could, but especially Europe. But Americans were by no means the only people interested in Euro-dollars; because they had the advantage of being instantly accepted in every country, and of not being subject to any central control, they appealed to businessmen in many other nations. Critics say the Euro-dollar has added to inflation, and has led to increased speculation. They look forward to the day when Europe introduces its own currency; if and when that happens, the role of the Euro-dollar will be severely diminished, if not ended altogether. Meanwhile, other Euro-currencies, notably the German mark, are increasingly challenging its position as the most generally accepted paper money. (See also EURO-BONDS and EUROPEAN MONETARY UNION.)

## EUROPEAN (THE)
A term which used to mean colonial administrator but now denotes someone who believes in the Common Market. Churchill had a vision, back in 1948, of the true European. 'I hope', he said, 'to see a Europe where men and women of every country will think as much of being European as of belonging to their native land, and wherever they go in this wide domain will truly feel "here I am at home".' The only people who are like that, in fact, are the Eurocrats in Brussels, the young men and women who prefer travel to a dull job at home, and the Americans who work in a European city. For a decade or so after the last world war, the Germans and, to a lesser extent, the Italians, tried to hide their shame by professing to be Europeans. With the war almost forgotten, they do so no longer. Nationalism has come into its own again. The young, on the whole, feel more at home in Europe than anyone else. They did not experience the last two wars, and care remarkably little about them. They do not see Germans or Italians as enemies, and are much more inclined to regard the beaches of Italy or France as common

property. Like Henry Ford, they tend to feel that history is bunk. Napoleon's battles have the same ludicrous ring about them as those old newsreel films of the Nuremberg rallies and other displays of patriotic fervour which inspired earlier generations. Europe looks a good deal smaller to the twenty-year-old of today than it did to his father and grandfather. It will look smaller still to *his* sons – though it will be a very long time before anyone introduces himself at a party with the words: 'Hallo, I'm a European.' To the Chinese, of course, all distinctions are academic: to them, all Europeans look the same.

## EUROPEAN MONETARY UNION
A concept cherished by those who believe that there's more to creating a United Europe than making pious speeches. The aim is an integrated money and capital market within the EEC, and a common currency. In other words, businessmen in EEC countries should be able to borrow wherever they like, without interference, and we should all be able to use the same kind of money. The Six have actually agreed on a three-stage plan towards full monetary union by 1980, but this is generally thought to be far too optimistic. The trouble is, as usual, that politicians find things much more difficult than the theorists. There has never been any shortage of plans; the only problem has been a shortage of desire to make them work.

The Common Market is the biggest trading bloc in the world, and it clearly makes sense to establish a European money market, and a European currency. There are frequent meetings between all the ministers concerned: there is even a European Parliament where, in theory, differences can be sorted out in a democratic manner. But individual countries, notably France, have not yet made up their minds what kind of Europe they really want. They want to enjoy the advantages which the EEC offers, but dislike the idea of handing over national sovereignty to a European body. Progress, therefore, has been slow. There have been useful steps, such as the creation of a European Currency Unit – defined in terms of gold to be the same weight as the dollar, and used in money-raising operations by bodies such as the European Coal and Steel Community. But as a rule, meetings to discuss really important moves have ended either in disarray, or in compromise solutions forced upon the EEC by some US initiative. Some experts think that Britain's entry into the Common Market will ensure faster progress: others argue that it will merely widen the scope for disagreement.

## EXCHANGE CONTROL

An official attempt to regulate the amount of money going in and out of a country. The motive is simple enough – governments are not content to leave the rate which a currency may command abroad at the mercy of free market forces. They may genuinely want to keep exchange rates stable, or they may think it advisable to operate with an undervalued currency in order to make exports competitive. Britain has long had an elaborate system of exchange control, and a full list of all the regulations would fill a separate book. Treasury and Bank of England officials responsible for administering it have admitted to me that even they don't know all of them. You can't have a bank account abroad without government permission, or use your own money to buy property anywhere outside the Sterling Area, unless the Bank of England gives official approval. You can't hold certain foreign securities, or buy gold, without special authority. I am giving you just a few of the more obvious examples: the whole exchange control field is a bureaucratic paradise.

Under the Common Market rules, we are supposed to get some major changes. One of the aims of the Common Market, after all, is to remove artificial barriers within Europe. Experience suggests, however, that officials are reluctant to give up entrenched positions and that politicians tend to give in to them. The public, on the whole, does not seem to care enough to apply real pressure. The only measure of exchange control which has caught the imagination, over the past decade, was the 1964–70 Labour Government's introduction of a £50 travel allowance. Jim Callaghan, the Chancellor responsible, has since told me that I put the idea into his head in a long article I wrote for *The Guardian*. It's enough to make one want to give up writing.

## EXECUTIVE

A man who talks to visitors while the employees get their work done.
'Executive' was once a high status word, designating the top people
in a corporation – from departmental heads upwards. Today it is
applied much more generously. Anyone whose office duties require
him to supervise the work of at least one other person has nowadays
some claim to being called an executive. A higher executive can
usually boast of a generous expense account, a company car, and a
key to the executive lavatory. But the boundaries are getting
blurred: expense accounts are not so difficult to come by, and even
the newest office recruit, sharing a secretary with a colleague, can
usually get away with calling himself an executive. He may have to
settle at first for 'junior executive', but this stage usually doesn't
last very long. Top management, anxious to keep ahead, usually
likes to be known as 'senior executives'. But the most coveted title
is chief executive: it's the one label which still means what it says.

Car manufacturers, airlines, railways, magazines and many others
have done their best to exploit the executive boom. You don't have
to be an executive to own an executive car, or to take an executive
trip. Or, for that matter, to read this – which is, of course, an
executive book.

## EXECUTOR

No one has yet devised an effective way of taking it with you, but
an executor will ensure that what you leave behind doesn't fall into
the hands of the wrong people. The first step is to make a will; if
that sounds morbid and defeatist, remember that we've all got to go
eventually and dying intestate (that is, without making a will) may
cause your relatives a lot of quite unnecessary trouble and expense.
A will allows you to select your own executor, and many people
automatically pick husband, wife, or grown-up son or daughter.
Another possibility is a family friend with experience in business,
finance or the law: a frequent choice is that of the solicitor who has
drawn up the will. The larger banks all have executor and trustee
departments who, like solicitors, will take on the job for a fee. If
you have reason to think that your relatives might fall out over your
money, it makes good sense to think in terms of an independent,

professional executor. Whatever you do, don't forget to tell him: he cannot be forced to act for you, and he would certainly take offence if you neglected to inform him in advance of what, in many cases, turns out to be quite an arduous duty.

An executor has no power to act until the High Court grants 'probate' – proof that the will is valid and official authority for him to proceed. He will do his best to carry out your wishes, but remember that a will can be challenged. A surviving husband or wife, an unmarried daughter, a son under twenty-one, and any children who cannot maintain themselves because of mental or physical disability can ask for reasonable provision to be made out of the estate.

## EXPENSE ACCOUNT

An arrangement designed to exploit human weakness for the benefit of the firm. The theory is simple: a bottle of champagne, a portion or two of caviar followed by *Mignon de Bœuf en Croûte Lutèce*, a bottle of *Château Lafitte*, and an obliging hostess in gownless evening strap are held to be more effective in capturing contracts for one's products than the quality, price, or speedy availability of the said products.

Sometimes this is actually true. But more often than not the expense account lunch, dinner, or late-night entertainment merely soften the client up for a deal which, one could argue, would be signed anyway. It is a debatable point. The Americans call expense account lunches 'eating meetings', and having attended quite a number I can vouch for the fact that a good deal of important business is conducted on these occasions. (Americans are much too obsessed with business to discuss anything else.) The Japanese, on the other hand, use expense accounts to finance the kind of binge which would be quite impossible on their salaries. I once announced, to a group of Japanese businessmen in Tokyo, that I would be interested in seeing the Ginza – Tokyo's night club district. Immediately, half-a-dozen volunteered to show me around. I took it to be an acknowledgment of my importance, but as the evening wore on I realized that I was simply an excuse. We went to a hideously expensive geisha party, at which my hosts delighted in crawling about on all fours, and playing pat-a-cake and musical chairs – with sabuton cushions substituted for seats. We had a lot of fun, but business was never mentioned.

In Britain, expense account living is less frantic, but certainly qualified as a tradition. An expense account is less of a status symbol than it used to be, but still confers a certain distinction. Some companies are more widely known for their parties than for their products. And some executives command the affectionate respect of their colleagues for their ingenuity in devising acceptable returns. The Labour Government of 1964–70 made a determined effort to clamp down on what, in their prejudiced wisdom, ministers dubbed 'grouse moor living'. It did so by changing the rules under which all expenses were tax deductible (i.e. could be paid out of the company's profits before corporation tax was levied); henceforth, it said, most of a firm's entertainment would have to be paid for out of a firm's profits after tax. It made life a little more difficult for junior executives, but expense account living at the top went on as before. British traditions are hard to destroy, and expense accounts go back to Sir Francis Drake, whose account books, itemizing his expenses in the year of the Armada, came up for auction not long ago.

The same, of course, is true of the United States, where George Washington set a splendid example during the War of Independence. American author Marvin Kitman, who wrote a book about it, says The Man Who Could Never Tell a Lie collected nearly half a million dollars expenses for routing the British. He used '42 basic principles of expense account writing', including many still used today. His fundamental principle, says Mr Kitman, was 'be specific on the smaller expenditures and vaguer on the large ones. Describe in some depth the purchase of a ball of twine, but casually throw in the line "dinner for one army". He also favoured the "escalation principle" – each entry should be higher than the former.' Washington's skill on the financial battlefield naturally makes one wonder why he fought us at all. Could it have been just for the money? Inevitably, too, Mr Kitman's revelations raise profound questions about other leaders. What did Napoleon's accountants say to him when he came back from Moscow, or Rommel's after Alamein?

# FACTORING

A financial service developed in the United States, and later adopted by Britain and others. It makes cash available to a client in exchange for his book debts. As soon as a factoring company's client despatches his products, or provides a service, to his customer, the 'factor' will immediately make cash available against the invoice value of those products or services. A 'factor' thus becomes the credit control department, looking after debtor accounts, book-keeping and collection, as well as providing a source of working capital in relation to the size of debts outstanding.

Many firms who use a 'factor' regard the service element as more important than the provision of finance. The factoring company is often the only readily available financial adviser apart from the banks, and so a 'family doctor' relationship develops.

It works even better where bank managers and factors work together for mutual clients; nowadays, the banks themselves are so closely involved with factoring that this is not at all difficult to achieve. The annual cost is based on the amount of work involved, the client's industry, product or service, and quality of customers. True factoring companies offer something called a 'non-recourse system of payments', which in plain English means they have no recall on their clients if they cannot obtain payment from the customers. Or, putting it another way, they accept the credit risk.

# FEASIBILITY STUDY

Trying to find out if something will work. A lot of business ideas sound absolutely splendid in theory, but turn out to be duds once you start putting them into practice. A feasibility study really amounts to doing a bit of homework before you charge off in this or that direction. You look at the market and try to assess what it will bear; you estimate the cost of launching and development; you try to work out the long-term prospects. I have done quite a number of these exercises myself and to an enthusiast like me it usually proves to be a rather depressing experience. I realize, though, that they have spared me from making some very costly mistakes. Feasibility studies are nowadays regarded as an essential preliminary to any venture, and rightly so. The chief danger is that accountants, lawyers and others may argue you out of what is really quite a sound idea. When all is said and done, business is bound to involve some risk. Homework, however thorough, can only take you so far. If you haven't the courage to go a step further you might as well join the vast army of people whose main qualification is that they know what *not* to do.

## FED (THE)

'The Fed' is short for Federal Reserve System, the central bank of the United States. The Banking Act of 1935 describes it as a 'public institution' – but it is not a formal branch of government nor a presidential agency. The system is made up of a Board of Governors, and advisory council, twelve federal reserve banks (representing the twelve federal reserve districts) and member banks. All national banks are members; state banks can choose whether they want to be or not. The Federal Reserve Board supervises banking activity, and has final authority over discount rates (corresponding to the British Bank Rate) and other interest rates. It also has power to regulate the supply of credit. In short, although it may not be a branch of the official government, it exercises considerable influence over public policy. This, of course, is true of most central banks.

The Fed's governors pride themselves on their independence and there are times when they and the Administration appear to be pulling in the opposite direction. A traditional complaint of all central bankers is that politicians encourage too much public spending and inflation, and that they are too slow in taking corrective measures, such as higher taxes. The orthodox banking answer is to restrict credit and raise interest rates, and this may sometimes lead to open clashes with the President of the day. In 1965, for example, William McChesney Martin, a man of decided views, challenged President Johnson's cheap money policy by raising the discount rate from 4% to 4½%. The success of this kind of thing depends almost as much on the personal standing of the man who heads the Board of Governors as on the authority of the Fed itself. But presidents do tend to have the last word: it is they who appoint and re-appoint him.

## FINANCIAL INCENTIVE
'If you're not in business for fun or profit', says Robert Townsend in *Up the Organization*, 'what are you doing here?' A good question, and one which most people ask themselves long before they have made their first million. The answer is, perhaps, less simple than is generally assumed. The profit motive is, unquestionably, a most powerful driving force. A million (or even a few hundred thousand) may not be the most important thing in the world, but it certainly helps to make life more pleasant. Money, someone once said, 'is the only substance which can keep a cold world from nick-naming a citizen "Hey you!".' But the financial incentive argument should not be overdone. Management experts will tell you that 'job satisfaction' is often more important than differences in financial rewards. Prestige, power, security, honours and – yes – fun! are far more potent influences than we tend to acknowledge. If it were not so, most millionaires would either retire or move to the Bahamas. Even fear can be more potent than financial reward; it's remarkable how often the threat of dismissal galvanizes an executive into action.

Tax cuts are frequently urged upon governments because, it is claimed, a little encouragement to make more money will make everyone work harder than ever before. It is an attractive theory, but I have always suspected that it is more effective as a political slogan than as an economic weapon. This is partly because the majority work to live, rather than live to work. But there is more to it than that. There is no evidence, either in Britain or America, that tax cuts alone lead to a really significant change in attitude towards work. They stimulate spending, but do not necessarily stimulate effort. One economic research organization found that, on the contrary, really ambitious people work harder under high taxation. They are determined to get the things they want, and if it takes more effort to acquire the necessary spending money they will do their best. Experience also shows that, as far as industry is concerned, the general economic outlook and the availability of credit can be at least as important as tax considerations.

## FIXED PARITY
The price officially set for a country's paper currency. Under the

85

system created at Bretton Woods every currency had a fixed relationship with the dollar, which in turn was linked to gold. Exchange rates were pegged at levels which were adjustable only when it became clear that circumstances had made them unrealistic. This, it was argued, ensured the people knew where they stood, and helped world trade. More recent developments have cast doubt on the value of this arrangement; many people consider it too rigid. (See also FLOATING and WIDER BANDS.)

## FIXED PRICE CONTRACT

An arrangement under which someone agrees to supply goods at a stated price. Considerable time may elapse between the ordering of, say, heavy machinery and its actual delivery. The customer would naturally like to be sure that it won't cost more than the figure originally quoted. He may, therefore, ask for a written guarantee, and if the supplier badly needs the business (as has been true of so many heavy equipment firms in recent years) he will oblige. But with costs, particularly wage costs, escalating all the time, it is a risky business. Even a modest increase may wipe out all the profit; and in the case of contracts to deliver in two or three years' time, the deal may actually result in a loss. Most manufacturers, therefore, try to build a clause into contracts which permits them to pass on unavoidable increases in production costs.

## FLIGHT FROM MONEY

What tends to happen in periods of rapid inflation, when people find that money buys less and less. The basic rules of the anti-money game are splendidly simple. One, don't hold on to money – spend it. It will be worth less tomorrow. Two, don't just leave your money in the bank, or in old-fashioned stocking-type investments. They also lose value. Three, look for more dynamic outlets – and borrow as much as you can in order to help finance what you are doing.

Like me, you probably wish you had a little more money to fly away from. For people like us the number one rule is to buy a house on borrowed money. The value of most properties in central locations has risen enormously over the years. I have no doubt that, if you choose wisely, even today's prices will seem low ten years from now. If you already own a house, a second home, in the country or at the seaside, may prove a good investment. The better-off go in for a wide range of anti-money devices, including speculation in commodities and investment in agricultural land. Paintings and antiques have a large and enthusiastic following, and some people invest in coins, rare books, oriental rugs, silver, porcelain – anything which is likely to keep its value better than paper money. (See TIMES-SOTHEBY INDEX.)

## FLOATING
Letting the price of currency be determined by the laws of supply and demand. The international monetary system set up at Bretton Woods during the Second World War provided for exchange rates to be fixed at internationally agreed levels. (See FIXED PARITY.) Stability, it was argued, would help world trade. It did. Economists, however, disliked the sacrifices which frequently had to be made in terms of economic growth for the sake of maintaining fixed rate. Britain, for example, was repeatedly forced to slam on the brakes in order to 'defend the pound'. Floating was said to provide more flexibility. Canada floated its dollar in 1950 as a 'temporary' expedient and stuck with it for more than a decade. In 1971, President Nixon initiated a move which, within weeks, led to the widespread floating of currencies. In most cases, rates were not completely free-moving. They were simply allowed to fluctuate by much more – 3% or even 5% – on either side of the agreed parity. This is known as a 'controlled float', and experience suggests that it is, in many ways, better than a system of rigidly maintained rates. At the time of going to press Britain had just decided to float the pound.

## FLOOR BROKER
Wall Street's term for someone who actually does the buying and selling on the Stock Exchange floor – as opposed to the customers' broker, who deals directly with the public outside. The word 'floor' is used in Britain, too, but you are more likely to be told that your

favourite broker is 'in the House'. The London system differs from Wall Street in that it has both brokers and jobbers – the latter being traders who actually make the market in the shares, buying and selling them from brokers. Like all middlemen, they make their profit out of the difference between the price at which they buy the shares and the price they sell them at. Brokers have to be fast on their feet; jobbers get around less, but have to think twice as quickly. Both are generally referred to as 'dealers'. On Wall Street, the nearest thing to a jobber is the 'specialist' – a broker who confines his activities to a group of stocks sold at one trading post. Wall Street also has the so-called Odd Lot Dealer and the 'two-dollar broker'. Stock are dealt in on the Stock Exchange in units of 100 shares; anything less (i.e. anything from one to ninety-nine shares) amounts to an 'odd lot'. The odd lot dealer performs a kind of wholesale function by breaking up round lots of stocks into smaller packages. The client pays the normal price for the stock, and normal broker's commission, but also has to pay a fee to the odd lot dealer for his services. The 'two-dollar' broker is one who makes his living by transacting business for other brokers on the floor of the Stock Exchange; he used to get two-dollar fees for every order carried out.

## FORWARD PURCHASE

Goods or shares are often brought forward when sizeable amounts are involved; it means the supplier undertakes to provide a stated quantity at a certain future date for a stated price. Such dealings may also be known as futures or options. In the foreign exchange market, forward dealings usually involve companies who want to protect themselves against exchange risks, such as the devaluation of a currency. A company which has a large contract to buy, say, a piece of machinery from Germany may enter an arrangement which ensures that the necessary currency will be supplied on the date payment is due, at the present exchange rate. (See also LEADS AND LAGS.)

## FOUNDATION

An institution, often named after its benefactor, which finances and controls worthy causes such as universities, libraries, art galleries, and scientific research. There are lots of millionaires, but the ones who really stand out are those who have managed to set up their own foundation: it is the status symbol *par excellence* in the world of the super-rich. If you endow, say, a college or university you can generally count on getting at least one doctorate in return; in Britain, you may also get a knighthood. But public gratitude and recognition need not be the only motive. Indeed, it sometimes is a minor consideration. Charitable foundations get very favourable treatment from the tax authorities, and are therefore a useful way of avoiding taxation. Among other things, they can be used to keep control of a corporation in the family. Estate duty and other taxes are frequently so high that when the principal stockholder dies his family has to sell large blocks of shares – and, in doing so, relinquish voting control. This can be avoided by granting or bequeathing shares to the foundation at an early stage.

Representative Wright Patman, who led a US Congress investigation into the whole subject in the early sixties, also found that foundations can become tax free receptacles for capital gains. The creator simply makes over property which has appreciated substantially in value. The foundation is free to sell the investment (no gains tax) and to lend the entire proceeds back to the donor at a nominal rate of interest. Alternatively, it may use the untaxed money to buy a sizeable share block in some company the original donor wants to control. With this control he can raise or lower the company's dividend rate, milk its large cash funds and otherwise re-arrange things to his own benefit.

## FRANCHISE

A way of making money without doing all the work. You think of a good idea, get it going, and then allow other people to have the franchise – to rent the idea from you. One obvious first step is to protect your invention by getting a patent (see page 141) and registering your trademark.

A well-known example of successful franchising is Colonel Saunders' Kentucky Fried Chicken chain, now also popular in Europe. He started with little more than a recipe, and travelled all over the United States selling concessions to hopeful small-time businessmen.

An essential safeguard, besides registering one's trademark, is to lay down fairly strict rules about what the people who buy franchises can or cannot do. An unscrupulous – or careless – operator can easily damage one's reputation.

## FREE ENTERPRISE

A system based on private ownership and minimal state interference. The Government is expected to provide a broad framework of laws on property, contract, patents and the like, but to resist the urge to plan, direct, and regulate. Adam Smith, a Scottish professor of philosophy, is widely credited with being the 'father' of free enterprise; Karl Marx is given credit for being its most influential critic.

Smith argued that man works best in his own self-interest; therefore he should be allowed to do just that. Out of each of us doing what is best for us individually, common good will flow. The businessman, Smith wrote in *The Wealth of Nations,* 'is led by an invisible hand to promote an end which was no part of his intention . . . by pursuing his own interest he frequently promotes that of the society more effectually than when he really intends to promote it. I have never known much good done by those who affected to trade for the public good.'

Well, that was in 1776, and it must have seemed like a very refreshing change from the feudalism of the previous centuries. It still holds great appeal for most businessmen, especially in the United States. 'Free' is a nice, emotional word and it is easy to believe in the virtues of a free market if things are going your way. In practice, though, we no longer have truly free enterprise.

In the nineteenth century the idea of free enterprise was increasingly attacked on the grounds that it led to exploitation of the working class. Market forces can be a cruel master. The Soviet Union and other countries turned communist; countries, like Britain, went in for a mixture of socialism and capitalism (see MIXED ECONOMY). Key industries were taken over, planning ceased to be a dirty word, and the market system was influenced in all sorts of ways.

The decline of free enterprise, though, also reflects at least in part the changing attitudes of businessmen themselves. They want freedom, but call for protection as soon as someone gets the better of them. They believe in self-interest, but insist on government action as soon as organized labour tries to apply the same principle. They agree that free enterprise means 'standing on your own feet', but readily accept government grants and subsidies.

To many Americans, President Nixon's price and wage controls seemed like the last straw: if the home of capitalism could go in for that kind of thing, what possible future was there for the market system?

## FUNDAMENTALIST

Wall Street term for analysts who like to make their investment decisions on basic facts: a company's record and current rate of profits, its competitive position within its industry, the state of the economy – in short, anything which is likely to affect its performance. The assumption is that, if you do your homework, not much can go wrong. The fundamentalist has little time for people who rely on guesswork, or for fellow analysts who believe that the study of charts – based on the behaviour of the market rather than on the basic merits of an individual company – are more likely to make you money. It sounds commonsense, and usually reduces one's risk. It's certainly the best policy if you are chiefly interested in long-term investment. But stock market prices are made by people, not statistics, and do not always obey the dictates of commonsense. Not everyone, moreover, is in agreement about which of the various 'fundamentals' count the most. Homework helps, but it does not guarantee a profit.

## GATT

Shorthand for General Agreement on Tariffs and Trade. One of the major talking shops in the free world, and an important provider of customers for Geneva hoteliers. The General Agreement was negotiated at Geneva in 1947, and is based on a number of worthy principles – non-discrimination in trade, negotiated reductions in tariffs (customs duties), and the gradual elimination of other barriers to trade, such as restrictive government buying policies, special export finance or quantitative restrictions on imports. The principles are constantly discussed, and often implemented. The so-called Kennedy Round, for example, resulted in many negotiated reductions in world tariffs. But principles often fall foul of financial realities, and GATT rules have been flouted with impunity on more than one occasion. In 1964, for example, Britain introduced an import surcharge – prohibited under GATT regulations – and kept it going despite protests from other nations. In 1971, the United States did exactly the same. The European Common Market has developed trading agreements which, strictly speaking, are against the principles of GATT and so has Japan. The trouble with GATT is that it depends entirely on the voluntary recognition that trade wars are bad for all concerned: it can condemn, but it has no teeth. Codes of conduct tend to look good on paper, but are a great deal less impressive when they have to pass the test of actual experience.

## GAZUMPING
Fashionable term for what, alas, is quite an old-established practice: breaking a 'gentlemen's agreement' (by which the British have always set such store) between someone who wants to sell his house and a prospective buyer. What happens is that, before legally binding contracts are exchanged, the seller pulls out of the deal – usually because he's had a better offer. It is, of course, possible for the other party to raise his own bid, but in many cases he simply cannot afford to do so.

Gazumping tends to be particularly widespread at a time when houses are scarce and money is plentiful. The upsetting part, from the buyer's point of view, is not only that he loses a house on which he and his family have set their heart, but that he has been involved in a waste of time and expense. A couple seeking a £5,000 loan from a building society stand to lose as much as £75 in legal and surveying fees and other charges if the seller pulls out. Efforts have been made to stop this kind of thing through parliamentary legislation. A simple self-help solution is to ask for written assurance from the seller, when agreement is first reached, that he will reimburse the cheated buyer if he should subsequently refuse to sell at the agreed price.

## GEARING

The relationship between a company's ordinary share capital (or equity) and so-called prior charge capital. The latter includes anything with a prior claim on the year's profits and on assets – loan stock, debentures, preference shares. If there's a high proportion of it, the company is said to be highly geared. The significance of this for investors is that high gearing increases the likelihood of fluctuations in dividends on ordinary shares. In good years, when profits show a healthy rise, the part available for ordinary shareholders jumps smartly. In bad years, when profits fall, the amount left over for them drops sharply and the dividend may be reduced. Many investors dislike companies with high gearing and stay clear of them. It's certainly a point worth watching out for if and when you're thinking of buying equities.

## GETTING THE COUNTRY MOVING AGAIN

No one quite knows who fathered this gem, or what it means. It has nothing to do with trains, redeployment, or emigration. Its main purpose is to cash in on the dissatisfaction of people who feel, for one reason or another, that they're in a rut. The late John F. Kennedy used it with great effect. Mr Wilson did so after him. And Mr Heath has copied Mr Wilson. 'Getting the country moving again' is a great favourite with Conference Man, and has a number of offsprings. One of the best-known is 'building a better Britain'. I'm not sure who is supposed to do the building, and what the end result is meant to look like. I do know, though, that we can do it because 'ours is still a great country and we are still a great people'. I know, too, that it's done by 'building on the solid achievements of the past' and by 'releasing the energies of the people'. The solid achievements of the past do not, of course, include anything achieved during the years when one's opponents were build ing the new Britain. Once you have done the releasing, you must 'get rid of the little men with small minds', and 'wage w ar on inefficiency'. The little men, needless to say, are not you and I, but the people next

93

door. And inefficiency, as we all know, is a sin for which we can safely blame the other fellow. You deal with it by pointing out that 'the world does not owe us a living', and by appealing to 'the spirit of Dunkirk'. I have no idea why this mysterious spirit is held to have such magic powers – I have always thought that people would prefer to forget about that episode – but then I am not a politician.

## GILT-EDGED

A phrase which goes back to the last quarter of the nineteenth century, and is supposed to mean 'absolutely safe'. Don't you believe it. The best-known 'Gilts' are Government stocks, and it is true that interest on them is paid with unfailing regularity and that fixed repayment dates are invariably honoured. But 'safe' is quite the wrong word, because it implies that you can't lose. The truth is that prices can, and do, fluctuate in this sector as much as anywhere else.

This is especially true of the undated stocks, so called because there is no specific commitment to repay at any given point of time. Many things can influence their market value: the general level of interest rates, the state of sterling, the rate of inflation, and so on. They have no redemption 'floor' to stop falls when interest rates are rising or there is a crisis of one kind or another.

*The Financial Times* Index of Government stocks reached a high point of 127·4 in 1935. Thirty-four years later, in 1969, it established a 'low' of 64·21. The most widely-held gilt-edged stock, War Loan $3\frac{1}{2}$%, is worth less than half the price at which it was originally issued, and has been lower still. So much for safety!

## GIRO

A system, operated by the Post Office, which offers a basic banking service. Anyone can open an account by depositing a sum of money at a post office. The account is kept at the National Giro centre, and if you want to transfer money to another person you simply write the details on a transfer form and post it to the centre. If he also has an account, the amount will automatically be transferred to it. If not, the centre will send him a payment order and he can cash this at a post office. It is also possible to transfer funds to a bank, rather than another Giro account, but for this there is a modest charge.

Giro was set up, primarily, to help people who have no bank accounts, and to 'get cash off the streets'. It's both cheap and simple. Even so, it has not been anything like as successful as its sponsors had expected. One reason is that the service relies on the posts; delays in crediting accounts or settling bills with long intervals before acknowledgements come back from the centre have plagued the system from the start. Another is that, if you want to collect more than £20 from your account – or to get your money from a post office you don't normally use – you have to send an application form to the centre and wait for it to come back. Finally, Giro isn't allowed to make overdrafts, and won't tide you over if your account should slip temporarily into the red. Many shops are wary of accepting Giro cheques because of this.

## GOLD
A soft, industrially unimportant metal that costs money to keep (it earns no interest, and has to be guarded) and which has no intrinsic value. A gold bar doesn't even *look* pretty. You can wind a strip of gold around your loved one's finger, but a sparkling diamond will do at least as well. Your dentist can shove a chunk of gold into your mouth to fill a tooth, but it's not half as good as a nice, healthy, wholesome tooth. A piece of cheese would be more valuable if you were stranded on a desert island. And if you tried to pay your gas bill with a gold nugget you would almost certainly be prosecuted. Under British law, ordinary citizens are not allowed to hoard gold.

William Jennings Bryon, who sought the Presidency of the United States in 1896, urged his fellow countrymen not 'to crucify mankind on a cross of gold'. Henry Ford called gold the most useless thing in the world. G. K. Chesterton said that 'the golden age only comes to men when they have, if only for a moment, forgotten gold'.

I heartily agree. Gold is not worth the slaughter and misery it has caused over the centuries, and the passions which it still arouses today. The gold rushes of the last century, glamourized by films and television, claimed countless victims. Winston Churchill's ill-advised decision to tie the value of our money to gold bullion in 1925

95

had much to do with the depression which developed in the thirties. Gold belongs to the past, not the future. It's a totally inappropriate symbol for the space age. To their credit the Americans, who have a vast amount of gold buried in holes like Fort Knox, are trying hard to escape the yellow peril. They have refused to raise the official price, and they are no longer dealing in the stuff. As long as people continue to distrust paper currencies, the mystique of gold is unlikely to disappear. But one would like to think that, by the end of the century, its power will be broken. We shall still be attracted by its aesthetic appeal, and future generations will proudly accept gold watches and fountain pens on retirement. With luck, though, we shall learn to ask one simple, astonished question: 'gold – who *needs* it?' (See CARAT SCALE.)

## GOLD RESERVES

Officially, a country's pile of gold and foreign currency reserves – needed to meet possible demands arising out of its foreign trade and financial transactions. There *are* actual gold bars in the vaults of the Bank of England, and shipments of gold frequently leave the country. But changes of ownership are, for the most part, book-keeping transactions. A Bank official may go round tying new labels on different piles of gold, but more commonly a country will be credited with this or that amount. Because it has been banker to the sterling area, Britain has always needed somewhat larger gold reserves than other European countries. Under the rules of the monetary system set up at Bretton Woods in 1944, the Bank of England – acting on behalf of the nation – has had to use these reserves to maintain the agreed price for sterling. There have been many currency crises since the Second World War, but we've had only two devaluations. 'Attacks' have, as a rule, been countered by using the reserves to meet demands for foreign currencies.

The cost, at times, has been massive. Between 1964, when the Labour Party won office for the second time since the Second World War, and the forced devaluation of sterling in 1967, the reserves were so persistently under pressure that the Bank of England took to 'cooking the books'. The reserves total announced once a month seldom represented a true and fair statement of what

96

we actually had in the kitty. The Bank deliberately concealed the real position because, it said, it was in the national interest to keep speculators guessing. This was relatively easy to do because, in addition to actual gold and foreign paper money, we had all sorts of credit lines at our disposal. America, the International Monetary Fund, and others had made vast sums available for 'the defence of the pound'. They could quite legitimately be counted as reserves, since they were readily available to meet demands. It was, therefore, simple enough to disguise a disastrous month for the reserves by announcing that there was a modest loss after drawing an unspecified amount of credit. The trouble with this kind of technique is that it leaves the door wide open to rumours and guesswork – and the guesses sometimes exaggerate the seriousness of the position.

Because the reserves can be so heavily influenced by the inflow and outflow of 'hot money' – short-term capital looking for the most profitable home – they tend to fluctuate wildly. Once confidence in a currency is restored, the 'recovery' can be swift and dramatic as the earlier decline. This is one of the reasons why it is wrong to judge a nation's financial state solely by its gold reserves. Another is that they are usually only part of its assets. Britain, for example, has always had huge investments abroad. Most of these are privately owned (factories, or holdings of foreign securities) and could not be shown in the reserves without forced acquisition by the State. Such acquisition is feasible only in dire emergencies, such as war, and therefore does not amount to an answer to short-term problems. It certainly is no excuse for complacency. A man does not sell his house and car to pay off an overdraft; if his bank manager wants him to reduce the loan, he tries to make repayments out of current income. But the existence of those assets does give the lie to the popular assumption that a nation is 'broke' when it runs out of gold reserves.

## GROSS DOMESTIC FIXED CAPITAL FORMATION

The total amount spent on replacing or adding to buildings, vehicles, plant, machinery and so on. Spending on maintenance and repairs is excluded. It's one of the more obvious measures of a country's progress, and therefore forms an important part of economic study. It's also one of the more mysterious, and therefore impressive, pieces of economic jargon. Don't let it frighten you: it's much simpler than it looks.

## GROSS NATIONAL PRODUCT

The chief object of worship in so-called materialistic societies, most of whose citizens don't have a clue what it means. In official economic jargon, it's 'the total value at current or constant prices of the annual flow of goods and services becoming available to a country for consumption and maintaining or adding to its material wealth'. Roughly translated, this means that it's the way economists like to measure material progress. If you want to equate it with the life of an individual, you'd say the GNP is the yardstick by which you tell how much you have done to secure a decent standard of living for yourself and your family, how far you have succeeded in providing for services like schools and hospitals, and how much you have done to gain a reasonably secure future. During the last few years, economic growth has become a more fashionable phrase. There has also been a tendency, in countries with a higher GNP than ours, to cast doubt on the sense of turning it into a modern God. In Japan, for example, some people scathingly refer to it as 'Gross National Pollution'. (See THE QUALITY OF LIFE, page 154). In Britain, the GNP has never enjoyed quite the same status as elsewhere. This is partly because many people prefer leisure to material wealth – a preference which infuriates economists, but is not difficult to defend on humane grounds. Young people, in particular, despise the GNP. The truth, as economists like to say, 'lies somewhere in between'.

## GROUP OF TEN

Also known, more informally, as the Paris Club. Perhaps the most important forum for discussing changes in the monetary system, because its members are the finance ministers and top treasury officials of the ten 'richest' nations in the free world – the United States, Britain, West Germany, France, Italy, Japan, the Netherlands, Canada, Belgium, and Sweden. Switzerland is not officially a member, but usually takes part in the group's lending operations.

The Group of Ten has no real structure or staff, and is therefore less unwieldy than, say, the International Monetary Fund. Meetings can be called as and when the need arises, and the Group has demonstrated its effectiveness on a number of occasions. It has, for example, fixed up mammoth loans for Britain, and taken the key decisions leading to the creation of 'paper gold'. Because it is a highly political forum, however, disagreements can be frequent – and heated. The French, in particular, frequently clash with the Americans and, to a lesser extent, the Germans and the British. Members are fond of accusing each other of being 'obstinate' or 'selfish' – meaning the other fellow is just as unwilling to make concessions as you are.

## GROWTH STOCKS
Shares in companies whose earnings – and assets – are increasing rapidly; for many investors, it is the highest of all accolades. Companies whose shares are rated in this way often pay out very little in dividends, preferring to 'plough back' as big a percentage of profits as possible so that they can continue their rapid rate of growth. The rate of return offered at any given market price is almost invariably low. Growth stocks suit people who are more interested in capital gain than immediate income. But beware: the label is so sought-after that exaggerated and misleading claims are often made on what, before long, turns out to be a disappointingly brief period of advance.

## HAMMERING
What happens to a member of the London Stock Exchange if he cannot meet his debts. It takes its name from a long-established ritual: an official (called a waiter – another hangover from the coffee house days) mounts a rostrum and announces the name of the cad to the other members. It's the only sure way of producing silence in the 'House' during trading hours. Hammering doesn't happen very often, and there's a Stock Exchange fund to protect customers from the consequences. Brokers sometimes fail because a big client

has let them down, but a no less common cause is their own over enthusiasm about a particular share or group of shares.

## HARD CURRENCY

One which is freely exchangeable in world markets, and which has a comparatively stable value. Gold used to be the principal 'hard currency' – it probably explains the tag – and in many places it still is. Among paper currencies, the dollar has long been the market leader. If you go to Moscow or Leningrad, you will find that the big hotels all have shops in which one can buy goods not available in Russian stores, providing one has 'hard currency'. Prices are usually expressed in dollars – which, according to the Kremlin, also happen to be the hated symbol of capitalism. When I was last in Moscow, a Russian friend told me the story of a Soviet couple from Kiev who walked into one of these shops, delighted with the unexpected array of goodies, and produced their Russian roubles. 'Roubles', they were curtly told, 'are no good. You must have dollars.' The husband looked puzzled, and then asked: 'And where can I get these dollars?'

Inevitably, there is a black market in hard currency. (The rouble, you will have gathered, does not qualify for this exalted status.) In Leningrad I was twice stopped in the street by young men who asked if I could sell them pounds, marks, or dollars. They offered more than double the rate available in the hotels. That's the great thing about hard currencies: everyone wants them. Duty free shops at many airports insist on payment in money other than their own; governments use this method to secure the currency needed to buy weapons made in, say, the USA. Many countries, including Britain and the United States, do not allow their citizens to hoard gold and some put stiff restrictions on the import and export of foreign paper currency. Travellers from hard currency countries should take care not to exchange too much of their own money; they may have difficulty changing whatever is left over at the end of their trip into dollars, pounds, or German marks.

## HEADHUNTER

The perfect middleman, or so it's said. He's a consultant (the business world has so many consultants that one sometimes wonders who does the buying and selling) and his job is to bring employer and talented employee together. You want a brilliant sales manager? Right, contact a headhunter. A new chief accountant? The headhunter will know where to get one. That, at least, is the theory. Armed with a list of your requirements, he will try to lure suitable candidates either by advertising the job without mentioning names – or by making a direct, but discreet, approach to someone working for a rival firm.

The headhunter, clearly, has to be a good judge of men and a skilful diplomat. Both employers and candidates are apt to tell lies. The employer may say, at the outset, that he wants 'the very best man available – a dynamic executive'. If you take him at his word, and present him with an able and ambitious young fellow, his first reaction is quite likely to be one of horror: how could anyone expect him to hire someone who, in five or ten years' time, might very well try to take away his job? What he *really* wants is someone who looks and sounds like a dynamo, but who is unlikely to provide any serious competition. The candidate, for his part, will naturally attempt to sell himself as vigorously as possible – and that, as a rule, means he will offer his own, highly individual interpretation of the truth.

The headhunter has to be good at reading between the lines. But that's not all: he usually needs to know a few rather nasty tricks of his own. He may, for example, parade a few unattractive applicants before his client in order to make another man appear appealing. The bad candidate will, in all probability, never guess that he is being used. Most successful headhunters will tell you that the best people, by and large, are the ones who do not apply. They do not need the job that's offered, and in many cases prove reluctant even to consider switching. If they are good, the challenge tends to prove irresistible. Moral: if you meet a headhunter, play hard to get. But not too hard.

## HEDGING
Protecting yourself against market risks. There are several different forms of hedging, but they are all based on the same principle – it pays to insure. The housewife is hedging if she stocks up with, say,

baked beans because she fears an early rise in prices. A businessman may hedge by securing rights to commodities or foreign exchange ahead of the date when he actually needs it. Stock market speculators may hedge by taking out options (see page 138) or spreading their money over totally different fields. In times of economic uncertainty, for example, gold or gold shares often prove to be a popular hedge. There are countless refinements to this game, but beware of getting too eager: there's always a danger that you will wind up with what is known in the business as a Mongolian hedge – an investment so well insured that both profit and loss are impossible, with at least part of your capital swallowed up by insurance premiums.

## HOT MONEY
One of the more picturesque bits of jargon, meaning short-term capital looking for the most profitable – or secure – home. 'Hot' because, unlike money invested in plant and equipment, it can leave a country as quickly as it comes. Banks, large industrial companies and others have a certain amount of liquid capital available at any given time, and some of this may either be held in foreign currencies (especially if their price is likely to be pushed up by revaluation) or deposited with a bank or other institution in the country concerned. Hot money inflows can give a substantial boost to a country's gold and foreign currency reserves, but governments and central bankers dislike it because it tends to make for artificial situations. It's happened to Britain more than once. Attracted by high interest rates, hot money has come into London in vast amounts, giving an impression of great economic and financial strength. The outflow, however, has tended to be just as swift – touched off by a cut in Bank Rate, a bad set of trade figures, or simply the emergence of a more attractive home elsewhere. The country, lulled into a false sense of security by the apparently impressive size of its short-term assets, has suddenly been faced with a crisis. From time to time measures are taken to discourage hot money flows: a favourite device, used by Britain in 1971, is to ban the payment of interest on extra deposits by non-residents.

## HYPERINFLATION
Hyper comes from the Greek, and means over, above, exceeding,

excessive. Used in this particular context, it means inflation which has got out of control. A more widely used term is runaway inflation. Journalists sometimes claim that Britain has experienced just this in recent years, but that's an exaggeration. The most obvious example is Germany's experience in the 1920s, and again in the period immediately following the Second World War. Inflation reached such a stage that paper money was, effectively, replaced as currency by cigarettes and chocolate, and the value of savings fell to nothing. It explains why Germans, to this day, fear inflation more than anything else.

## IN-PLANT FEEDING SITUATION
Canteen lunch. The jargoneers have even taken over this apparently simple and straightforward part of the business scene. A recent survey of canteen lunches produced not only the above gem, but also 'corporate feeding plan' and 'total environmental conceptual thinking' – which, in plain English, means that the present type of works canteen may soon be replaced by leisure centres offering not only food, but also discothéques, supermarkets, and ping-pong.

## INCOMES POLICY
An attempt to influence prices, wages, and the level of employment by getting people to cooperate in a planned programme, rather than leaving it all to market forces. It sounds fine in theory and is a subject of endless speculation among economists. If only workers would realize that a free-for-all in wages leads, in the end, to higher unemployment . . . if only people would accept that the answer to inflation is joint effort . . . if only employers would realize that, if workers are to exercise restraint, companies must keep down prices. . . .

A prices and incomes policy has been tried in many countries. Sweden was one of the pioneers. In Britain, Harold Macmillan's Government set up a National Incomes Commission, but the whole enterprise came to nothing because of the traditional class division between workers and employers.

The 1964–70 Labour Government seemed, at first, to be more successful. Both sides of industry signed a 'declaration of intent', and the Government set up a National Board for Prices and Incomes with the specific brief of examining particular cases of prices and incomes behaviour and deciding whether they were in the national interest or not. Much publicity was given to splendid sounding 'productivity agreements'. In the end, though, the Government destroyed its case by constantly slamming on the brakes (and, in the process, raising prices through increases in tax) in order to defend the pound. The public began to feel cheated, and trade unions stepped up their efforts to get more money because, they claimed, price controls had failed.

When the Conservative Government won power in 1970, it promptly abolished the Prices and Incomes Board, and reaffirmed its faith in free market forces. It led, predictably, to high unemployment and a slowing down in the pace of inflation. But some ministers quickly recognized that, in a modern capitalist economy, cooperation is the only politically acceptable course of action. It may be more awkward, and certainly causes more argument, but it is also more just. Ironically, President Nixon recognized the need for a prices and incomes policy just as Britain, which had tried so hard to make it work, decided to play it down. An elaborate machinery was set up to operate it. I was in the United States at the time, and it all looked so familiar – the angry letters to newspapers and politicians, the arguments on TV, the charges of cheating, the protest marches with slogans like 'freeze the war, not wages'. There were councils and commissions – but, as we've had cause to find out in Britain, they do not by themselves add up to an effective incomes policy. Wages apart, how do you control prices in four million rental units? How can a seven-man price commission decide what is a fair profit, and what isn't, and how can it enforce its rulings?

Incomes policies will continue to fascinate economists – and governments – for many years to come. They are not the perfect answer to inflation, or to unemployment, but they are certainly more sophisticated than the more traditional weapon – fear. I doubt if they will ever prove 100% successful. They certainly won't work if politics, and deep-rooted class hatred, have too strong a hold. But they are a major economic weapon, and will continue to be studied – and applied—with the seriousness they deserve.

## INCREMENT
Genteel way of saying 'increase'. Civil servants and teachers, traditionally, do not get increases in salary but 'increments'. Many jobs have built-in annual increments. Employees are not expected to ask for a penny more: the whole point of the exercise is to avoid the embarrassing, working-class strategy of threatening to go on strike in order to get more money. The trouble is that, at times of rapid inflation, the poor white-collar chap who's stuck with 'annual increments' tends to be left behind everybody else. It's a high price to pay for a bit of out-of-date snobbery.

## INFLATION
A fall in the value of money due to rising prices – or, as someone once said, the equivalent of looking at your savings through the wrong end of a telescope.

The two main types are cost-push inflation, meaning that rising costs are the chief driving force, and demand-pull inflation, meaning that too much money is chasing too few goods. A modest degree of inflation is held to be a good thing, but runaway inflation is a menace. It represents the greatest threat to our individual and collective prosperity. If this is not always realized it is because, on the surface, inflation has many attractions. A worker who secures an increase in wages, automatically assumes he has bettered himself. He recognizes that the result is likely to be passed on to his firm's customers, in the form of higher prices, but consoles himself with the thought that this is none of his business. What happens, of course, is that the firm's price increase makes another worker, in another industry, ask for more money on the grounds that the cost of living has gone up. If he gets it, and that firm puts up its prices, the chap who started it all will ask for another increase on the grounds that the cost of living has gone up. And so on, and so on. This rather superficial impression of progress is also seen on a national scale. It is relatively easy to make people feel, in periods of inflation, that everything is going splendidly. Economists who warn of the dangers tend to be dismissed as jeremiahs who are always wrong. Politicians, as a rule, go along with the public mood, because it pays them to do so. In the end, of course, comes the reckoning.

The country which fears inflation most is Germany. Twice this century the Germans have had periods when money lost value so fast that the whole money-exchange system broke down. People were broke with lots of money in their pockets – and it wasn't funny. Just after the last World War, barter more or less replaced coins and bits of paper. Confidence in them broke down so completely that the country went, in effect, on to the 'chocolate standard'. Chocolate bars, packets of cigarettes, and tins of coffee were the generally accepted medium of exchange. They passed from hand to hand, just as paper money had done before. I happened to be there at the time and I well remember the reverence in which I – a young boy – held a chocolate bar. It never occurred to me that it had originally been made for eating: in my eyes, it was money.

## INFRASTRUCTURE

The services which form the basis of a modern economy – power stations, roads and railways, education, and so on. Private enterprise has played an important role in the creation of many infrastructures; British investors, for example, financed much of the railway development in South America. But nowadays state finance tends to play a much bigger role. Under-developed countries (or, as most prefer to be called, developing countries) are suspicious of what they regard as foreign exploitation.

In both India and South America I have been told by ministers that they would rather make slower progress than have American or British companies take over. They will readily give contracts to foreign firms, and accept aid and loans from other countries, but they are determined to keep control of each operation. In many cases, existing foreign investment has been nationalized – a fact which, inevitably, has scared off potential new investors. An American or British firm will, nowadays, be reluctant to invest big money in a country like India unless it can count on getting its money back within, say, five years. This means even less foreign investment. Left-wing or nationalist governments do not seem much bothered by all this: they look more concerned with appearances than with results. It would, very often, make much more sense to welcome foreign firms, let them build large factories, and then take them over.

Perhaps the worst feature of this whole business of creating infrastructures is that it generally means some sacrifice of individual liberty and effort. Stalin, for example, held back production of consumer goods (and punished those who didn't like his strategy) because he felt that the task of building up basic industries deserved priority. Some people say that, in effect, he 'wrote off' a whole generation. Future generations should benefit, but the morality of this sort of thing is obviously debatable.

## INSPIRATIONAL DISSATISFACTION

An absolute must, we are told, if you want to develop PMA – a Positive Mental Attitude. You simply won't get anywhere, the theory goes, unless you are dissatisfied – wholesomely dissatisfied. The trick is to turn it to your advantage. To do this, says Jack Lacy, who runs 'sales clinics' for the National Sales Executives Clubs, you 'push the hot button'.

How do you find the button? Well, 'you must discover what a person wants – and how you can help him to get it. The first thing you must do is to help him to crystallize a need in his mind for something he doesn't have. Then you show him that you have the best thing to fill that need. And when his desire becomes a burning desire, the person's hot button has been pushed'.

It helps, apparently, to have a problem. Every adversity, we are assured, has the seed of a greater benefit. A guilt feeling is also useful: 'it even motivates persons of the highest moral standards to worthwhile thought and action'. Indeed, failure is considered an essential pre-requisite to success and the greatest misfortune which can befall anyone is to have gone through life without encountering any problems.

I don't know about you, but I'm glad to say I'm not too badly off on this score. Why, then, am I not rich like so many authors of 'inspirational' books? The reason, I suspect, is that I do not always obey all the rules. W. Clement Stone and Napoleon Hill, the authors of a book called *Success Through a Positive Mental Attitude*, say one of the most important things to remember is always to 'add something more'. This amounts to adding the extra bit others have missed. For example, there was once a song writer who wrote a song but couldn't get it published. George M. Cohan bought it and added the three little words: 'Hip, Hip, Hooray!' The extra bit made him a fortune.

## INTERNATIONAL MONETARY FUND

A Special Agency of the United Nations, set up by forty-five countries after the Second World War with the aim of preventing a recurrence of the disastrous events of the thirties, when competitive devaluations and trade restrictions led to a slump in world trade. The Fund became the guardian of the free world's monetary system, and its articles of agreement provided an important framework of rules for exchange rates, balance of payments policies and other key factors. Each member contributed a quota of gold and its own currency, and this formed a pool from which the Fund made medium term loans to countries with balance of payments difficulties. It meant, in effect, that countries with temporary problems had an alternative to drastic measures which could harm the general level of international trade.

During the sixties, Britain repeatedly borrowed huge sums from the Fund, in order to defend the prevailing parity of the pound. The Fund's managing director, Pierre Paul Schweitzer, was dubbed 'Britain's bank manager', but he described himself as 'just a hired hand'. Real power, he pointed out, lay with the finance ministers who put up the money.

## INSTITUTIONS

Insurance companies, pension funds, investment trusts, unit trusts and other financial establishments which help to make up 'the City'. There are still individuals who count for a great deal – Lord Cowdray is a typical example – but the big institutions are now far more important than any single personality, however wealthy.

In an average week some £30 million of new money is available for investment by life assurance offices and non-government pension funds alone. Not so many years ago the rate was under £20 million a week. Then there are the unit trusts. Save and Prosper alone has

over £400 million in British ordinary shares – a figure which would
have been quite unthinkable twenty years ago.

It means that the unit trust movement, like other institutions,
possesses an immensely powerful weapon in the form of voting
rights. The one time when this power is clearly seen to operate is
during a takeover fight. On more normal occasions the City prefers
to work behind the scenes; public clashes, it is reasoned, are undignified and expensive, and tend to make the City appear arrogant
and heartless. Until fairly recently, most institutions would rather
sell a company's shares than get involved in its problems. But
getting out has become increasingly difficult, chiefly because institutions are so much more heavily committed to individual companies. There is, today, a much greater willingness to stay put and
to do something about a bad situation. 'Obviously', says the investment manager of one of the biggest insurance groups, 'we try to
step in at a fairly early stage. Most of industry is nowadays run by
managers, rather than the old-style owners, and an institutional
shareholder can usually play a decisive role in any boardroom
battle. As a rule, it's enough to go and see a company board, and to
make certain suggestions. If they are obstinate, and insist on making
a public issue out of it, we always sit down and reconsider our
position. If we can sell, we may try to do so. If not, we have to
decide whether to risk an open clash. Fortunately, it doesn't often
come to that.'

One snag, of course, is that one tends to come up against friends
and acquaintances. Multiple directorships are the rule rather than
the exception, and a single attack may give offence to a number of
people. The investment manager of one insurance company, for
example, will be reluctant to criticize a board which has powerful
backing from another insurance firm or from a merchant bank.
Even this, however, is gradually breaking down. The City is getting
more professional and more aggressive. Friendships, like old school
ties, count for less than they used to.

## INVISIBLES
Payments by individuals or firms of one country to those of another
which do not involve the physical movement of goods across

frontiers. They include earnings from banking, shipping, insurance, commodity markets, civil aviation, interest on overseas investments, and travel. The performance of a British play on Broadway, the shipping of foreign goods in a British ship, advice given to foreign clients, royalties paid to the Beatles, buying of British industrial 'know-how' by a foreign firm – all these things earn money which is no less important to our overall balance of payments position than exports of washing machines or bicycles. The City of London, obviously, plays a key role in this field. But 'invisibles' also include profits remitted from factories which British firms have set up abroad in order to jump tariff barriers or to satisfy the nationalist feelings of foreign governments. When this happens, the UK parent often stops direct exports – to the detriment of our published trade figures. But we are, in effect, still earning foreign exchange from its efforts. (See BALANCE OF PAYMENTS.)

## JOBBING BACKWARDS
A Stock Exchange term, roughly translated as being wise after the event. A popular sport in most professions, especially stockbroking and financial journalism. It's relatively easy to see, three or four years later, where one went wrong. A common cause is over optimism, but people usually manage to blame other factors – government action, the lack of reliable statistics, the foolishness of official forecasts, and so on. Jobbers – the people who act as intermediaries between buying and selling brokers – are as fond of indulging in this as everyone else. Jobbing backwards usually starts with the words 'if only . . .' and ends with the cosy assertion that one won't fall for it twice. Alas, a great many people do.

## JOB LIAR
For once, it means just what it says – but then it's not a scientific term. The great majority of us, an occupational psychologist called Ivor Goldstein found in a 1972 survey, lie about our qualifications when job hunting. Some even invent previous jobs.

Goldstein found that only one in four applicants lie about the title of the previous job, but from there on the 'discrepancies' really build up. The lying rate on salaries is prodigious – nearly 75%. The average exaggeration runs around 10% but some embellish their earnings by anything up to 25%. On length of time in the previous job, the average person will extend this by six months or more. But it's not unusual for an extra year or year and a half to be added on.

Goldstein says some employers are getting worried enough about these 'exaggerations' to take them into account when making appointments, and to increase checks. Liars, beware.

## KENNEDY ROUND
One of the more enlightened periods of haggling over tariffs on international trade which take place, from time to time, in Geneva, Switzerland. It was, in essence, an attempt to speed up reductions by replacing bargaining over rates on individual commodities by general cuts on most or all of them. The US and the Common Market confronted each other for the first time, but altogether fifty-three countries took part. The debate was tough and exhausting, but in the end it was agreed to cut tariffs throughout the Western world by an average of 27%. The Kennedy Round was generally seen as a decisive defeat for protectionism. (See also GATT.)

## KEYNES
John Maynard Keynes (1883–1946) was the most influential economist of his generation and possibly of this century. Educated at Eton and King's College, Cambridge, he was a brilliant student in mathematics, politics and philosophy. He eventually turned to economics in order to prepare for a civil service examination, and in 1906 entered the India Office. Two years later Keynes accepted a lectureship in economics at Cambridge, and during the First World War he did important work in the Treasury. The result was a highly successful book, *The Economic Consequences of the Peace*. His biggest impact, however, came with the publication of his *General Theory of Employment, Interest and Money* in 1936. The timing could not have been better: after the great depression, economic theorists were in disarray and desperately needed a saviour. Keynes adopted basic premises a little closer to reality than those of his predecessors. He argued against *laissez-faire*, and made a strong case for

government intervention, to compensate for the uncontrollable vagaries of private capitalism, even if it meant governmental deficits. He advocated a permanent policy of keeping interest rates low, and put heavy emphasis on the need to maintain full employment. His theories were by no means universally accepted, but his policy suggestions were practical enough (as well as correctly timed) to be widely adopted by politicians in desperate search of solutions. Keynes gave economics a new lease of life, and his views still command a very wide following today – although, inevitably, some of his arguments are increasingly challenged. Keynes was a skilful writer, but his *General Theory* is hard going for any layman. No matter; what counts is his ideas had, and still have, practical value. Keynes was not only a brilliant thinker; he also proved himself a highly successful stock market speculator. You can't ask for much more, can you? (See PUMP PRIMING.)

## LAISSEZ-FAIRE

Literally 'Let do', a French phrase used by economists to sum up the classical doctrine that 'the market' always knows best. Supporters of *laissez-faire* argue that the free pursuit by individuals of their own interests is likely to produce the greatest amount of wealth for a nation. State interference is not only unnecessary, but positively bad. The doctrine had a particularly strong hold in the nineteenth century – and that, as far as I'm concerned, is where it belongs. Even Mr Heath's government, with its much publicized demand that people should 'stand on their own two feet', accepts that it is out of date. It's generally recognized that the government has a right – indeed, a duty – to direct the use of resources in the interest of the community and to use the tax system to ensure a fair distribution of income. If unemployment reaches a socially unacceptable level, ministers cannot shrug their shoulders and say that free market forces must be allowed to take their course. If they do, they soon find themselves out of office. Even in the United States, the home of capitalism, *laissez-faire* has been rejected by the Nixon administration, which took the unusual step, in 1971, of announcing machinery for controlling the level of wages and prices.

## LAME DUCKS

Tory jargon for companies which don't pay their way, and are propped up by public funds. Virtually unheard of until the Tory Government started shooting some of them. When they ran out of profit and money, ministers allowed them to go bankrupt rather than provide a subsidy. Judged strictly in terms of profit and loss, Britain is full of lame ducks. Indeed, during the sixties the rest of the world would have readily accepted that description for the country as a whole. An accountant would find it easy to argue that the whole of Scotland is a lame duck – or, for that matter, most of Wales. The same goes for countless institutions. Theatres, opera companies, newspapers, airlines, nationalized industries like coal and steel – they all fail the test. So does the Monarchy; there is convincing proof that the Royal Family is not paying its way, and will continue to need substantial public support.

There are, of course, certain public services, such as electricity and water, which have to be protected no matter what. We have long passed the point where your electricity could be cut off overnight because the local supplier has gone bust. As long as we have proof that the industry is reasonably efficient, we willingly accept that it must occasionally make a loss. But this still leaves purely commercial organizations. Advocates of free enterprise argue that they should be left at the mercy of market forces. Others disagree: they say the social, industrial and economic consequences of major business crashes, especially in areas of traditionally high unemployment, are too great.

The only sections of the community totally free from sordid commercial considerations are ministries like the Treasury and the Foreign Office, which many people would consider to be very lame ducks indeed. We have no way of measuring whether they show a profit or loss. And how about the Army? Or the Navy? How do you judge their viability? By the number of enemies killed? Certainly not. Then how? By the number of wars avoided? May be. But that is hardly an argument which would commend itself to a stern accountant. How do you show something that hasn't happened on the assets side of a balance sheet?

## LEADS AND LAGS
A process which can, and usually does, have a major effect on the
strength or weakness of currencies, especially at times of crisis. A
company which regularly imports goods from Japan, for example,
and has reason to think that these goods may be made more expensive by a revaluation of the yen, will try to take precautions by buying Japanese currency well ahead of time. Similarly, a Japanese
company which regularly imports from Britain and which expects
either a revaluation of the yen or a devaluation of the pound will
delay making payment for as long as possible in the hope that the
goods will become cheaper in terms of the yen. The first is a 'lead',
the second a 'lag'. Given the importance of exports to both countries,
it is obvious that this kind of action can make a considerable impact.
It certainly did during the months preceding Britain's 1967 devaluation: every sensible industrialist tried to protect himself as far as
exchange control regulations allowed. (See FORWARD PURCHASE.)

## LEAKS
Disclosure of information by means other than an official statement.
Often, but not always, unintentional. A financial journalist may hear
that a particular company is to get a massive, highly profitable new
government contract. Or that Whitehall is sponsoring a new wave
of mergers in a particular industry. In each case, share prices are
bound to be affected. And he's got the story first. The minister or
civil servant who has leaked the information frequently does not
realize its potential value. Or he falls into traps set by ingenious,
scoop-hungry reporters. Most City leaks centre on takeover bids.
A lot of people tend to be taken into the chairman's confidence once
an approach has been made. They include directors, accountants,
outside advisers – and, inevitably, their wives. The temptation to
gossip, or even to make money out of the situation, is always strong.

There are many other types of leak – some designed to blacken
reputations, some to influence decisions which are about to be
made, some to affect share prices during a takeover fight, and some
to let the public know what a great guy the leaker is. Leakmanship
is a much more popular art than is generally realized. In Fleet
Street it is more commonly known – and praised – as a scoop. And

the biggest, if not the most expert, leakers of all can be found in the government. Ministers constantly leak information to the press. They talk 'off the record', which means the stuff can be used as long as you don't say who told you – a device which enables the government to issue a denial if the leak proves embarrassing. Occasionally they also tell you things which are 'for background only' – not for repetition, which is the official equivalent of 'strictly between you and me'. One advantage of this particular form of leakmanship is that ministers can 'test public opinion' without actually committing themselves to a certain course of action. It is also a way of applying pressure on, say, a foreign power without making a public statement.

## LEASING

One of the more interesting branches of finance – it means the renting out of all types of plant and equipment. Many firms find it more convenient to lease equipment rather than tie up capital in expensive fixed assets. They can do so by going to a finance company or bank, many of whom undertake just about every conceivable type of operation, from leasing oak casks for whisky maturing to leasing aircraft. Some specialize in tailoring their leases to fit particular requirements, especially for large contracts. They can equip complete factories, leasing everything down to typists' chairs.

Don't confuse leasing with short-term hire or contract hire, or rental provided by suppliers and manufacturers of such items as light commercial vehicles, earth-moving equipment, accounting machines, computers and the like. A leasing agreement is usually divided into two periods, primary and secondary. The total period can be as long as ten years. The primary period varies from three to seven years; during this period, the rental reflects the value of the equipment, and if for any reason you should want to cancel the deal, you will have to allow for rentals still unpaid. The secondary period can also be from three to seven years. Rentals are nominal and termination can take place without the need for further payment; the period can be extended at will.

Since leasing is a financial operation the lessee is usually responsible for maintenance, insurance, and all running costs.

## LIMIT ORDER

One of the ways in which an investor can keep control over the price he pays for shares. A lot of people simply ask their brokers to buy a particular stock which they think will go up. This is really a request to buy 'at the market', which means the dealer will buy the number of shares asked for at the best price he can get. With a widely traded stock this is a reasonable enough approach, but in many other cases it is more sensible to give buying and selling limits.

Share prices do sometimes change quite sharply within a matter of minutes or hours, especially if there are rumours of a takeover bid or if the shares have been strongly recommended by someone with an influential following. A limit order gives your broker flexibility. If you are buying, he must not buy at above the price you give. If you are selling, he must not sell at below the price you give. It's a lot better than telling him that, say, you want a share you've seen recommended at £2. The chances are that other investors have also seen that tip and the price will be higher by the time your broker or bank manager, however smart he may be, gets around to carrying out your instructions. The broker or bank manager then has to go through all the trouble of contacting you and telling you that there are no shares on offer at £2 and that the price is now so much higher. Unless you are quick, the chances are that the price will be still higher by the time your new instructions are carried through. How much better all round it would have been to have said at the outset to buy at £2, or nearest you can get to this, with a limit of such and such a figure.

## LITTLE MEN WITH LITTLE MINDS

Like lame ducks, they are always the fellow next door. The little men with little minds are people who, according to our politicians, must be disposed of as part of the 'war against inefficiency'. It's all part of the free enterprise philosophy and makes excellent sense to economic experts. The trouble is, however, that the little men with little minds have a vote like everyone else. And although they enthusiastically applaud the principle that everyone must learn to 'stand on his own two feet', they do tend to get a little difficult when it turns out that the people who propound this theory actually mean *them*.

## LIQUIDITY RATIO

The proportion of total assets which British banks conventionally hold in so-called 'liquid' items, such as cash and money which can be recalled at short notice. The figure nowadays is 28%, but some try to keep it a bit higher. The actual amount of cash in the till is very much less; even if one includes the money they have on account with the Bank of England (whose headquarters are just around the corner from the head offices of the big commercial banks) it doesn't add up to more than 8%. But customers have no need to worry. Banks are more than capable of meeting any normal demand. Only a major loss of confidence would create a 'run' on a bank, and if that were to happen to any of the big names (which is highly unlikely) the rest of the financial world would be more than willing to help out. It couldn't afford to do anything else.

## LONG-TERM

A convenient phrase if one wants to explain why an investment has turned sour. When critics howl for your head because, say, a share you have recommended drops by 50%, you calmly point out that you advised them to 'buy for the long-term'. This can be anything up to sixty years – by which time you will all be dead.

The City has many other devices for hedging one's bets, or passing the buck. There's no need, for example, to commit yourself to embarrassingly precise market forecasts. You can say that the market is likely to 'move sideways', or that it is 'bound to fluctuate a good deal during the coming months'. You can suggest that this is 'a tricky period for forecasting, perhaps more tricky than usual', and go on to say that 'we are, perhaps, approaching a turning point'. You can urge investors to 'watch out for opportunities to pick up bargains', or to be 'highly selective', without actually telling them where the bargains are, or what to select. If things go wrong, you can blame shakeouts, speculative excesses, and 'technical factors'.

## LOSS LEADER

Retailer's term for goods deliberately sold at a loss in order to attract customers. Bread and sugar are often used as loss leaders. They are essentials, and price-conscious housewives tend to be attracted by notices which offer them at an obviously favourable price. Supermarkets are particularly fond of using this technique, because they know that, once inside, the customer is likely to buy a lot of other goods on which they make a bigger profit. Manufacturers of goods with well-known brand names don't like the practice, because it tends to undermine the whole price structure. Under the Resale Prices Act of 1964 they can lawfully withhold goods from any retailer who has been using their product as loss leaders. Threatening to do often proves effective, but supermarket chains have increasingly taken to producing their own brand names, or signing up with a manufacturer who in return for a large and steady contact will go along with boardroom policy. Loss leaders, therefore, are here to stay.

## LOWER SOCIO-ECONOMIC STRATA
Working class. It sounds much more acceptable, doesn't it?

## MALTHUSIAN DOCTRINE
Named after a clergyman called Thomas Robert Malthus, who began to worry about the population explosion long before any of today's worriers were born. His *Essay on the Principle of Population*, published anonymously in 1798, caused a heated controversy. He devoted the next five years to further study of the subject, and in 1803 brought out a new edition much longer than the original, this time under his own name. The Malthusiasm doctrine is simple: unchecked breeding of man causes population to grow by geometrical progression, whereas the food supply cannot grow so rapidly.

'I think', wrote Malthus, 'I may fairly make two postulates. First, that food is necessary to the existence of man. Secondly, that the passion between the sexes is necessary, and will remain nearly in its present state.' Man, he suggested, could apply the remedy by prudence and self-restraint, just as he could avoid illness due to gluttony or drunkenness. He advocated late marriage, which he maintained would be good for human character and for the institution. Everyone should resolve to have no more children than he could support. This moral code, he felt, should be reinforced by society, through the simple expedient of refusing charity or public support to any families which could not support themselves. It seemed a harsh prescription for a clergyman to advocate, but Malthus justified it on the grounds that it was the only humanitarian remedy in its ultimate effect, shortsighted benevolence being a palliative which could only make the situation worse. It was Malthus' doctrine, and his solutions, which first earned economics the label 'dismal science'. His forecasts have failed to come true in the Western world, largely because of substantial increases in agricultural and industrial productivity which he did not foresee. But Malthus has had a considerable effect on economic and social thinking, and many economists still echo his views today.

## MARGIN BUYING
A method, popular on Wall Street, which allows you to buy stocks without putting down the full purchase price. The 'margin', in this case, is the amount you put down as a deposit. The rest is financed by the broker, who charges interest on the loan. Margin buying has obvious appeal to people who like to speculate, and was one of the chief factors behind the great crash of 1929. At the time, money was easily borrowed and you could secure ownership of a stock by putting down 10% of the purchase price or even less. A lot of people margined themselves up to the hilt, and were ruined when the whole deck of cards collapsed. Ever since, the Federal Reserve Board has had the power to decide what percentage deposit has to be paid to the broker: it has varied from 50% to the full 100%. The idea, clearly, is to prevent excessive speculation. But there are other deterrents. Interest rates, for example, often tend to be so high that the game isn't worthwhile unless you can afford to deal in very large amounts. Another snag is that, if you have a margin account, your broker keeps the shares as collateral. It should be okay, and usually is. But brokers are not infallible, and they do manage occasionally to lose stocks – and even to go bust. An alternative to margin buying are options. (See page 138.)

## MARKET CAPITALIZATION
The overall value which the stock market places on a company's ordinary shares. To discover what it is you multiply the number of

shares a firm has on the market by their present price. A company with a million shares priced at 250p each has a market capitalization of 250p × 1 million = £2½ million. Where a company has two or more types of ordinary share on issue – which happens in cases where a company wants to restrict voting rights of some share-holders – you add the capitalization of each class together to give a single figure.

Financial journalists are fond of dramatizing rises and falls in share prices by using market capitalization. In these days of giant corporations you may have a well-known name, like ICI or Courtaulds, with vast numbers of ordinary shares on the market. A quite modest fall in price, therefore, may produce the startling headline: 'millions of pounds wiped off the value of ICI'. It never fails to alarm the ordinary investor with, perhaps, 1,000 shares whose 'loss' may work out at a mere £50 – and who, in any case, may 'gain' it all back tomorrow when the shares recover.

## MARKET RESEARCH

Answer this question – do you like this book? If not, why not? What kind of book would you like to have bought instead? Then why on earth didn't you? When did you last beat your wife? If not, why not? What do you think of market research? Do you (a) find it a waste of time, (b) think it's the only way to sell, (c) don't know what it's all about?

Market research is a boom industry because everyone is seeking reassurance drawn from the law of averages. Businessmen, politicians, advertisers, and newspaper proprietors consider it easier and safer to follow the rest. They all feel they have a USP (unique selling proposition, in case you didn't know) but are afraid of setting the pace. The old-style entrepreneur is dead; the emphasis today is on scientific decision making based on the collection and evaluation of appropriate facts. Market research started with the mention of finding out who bought a particular product and why. It has since advanced to the point where products are designed to fit in with the researcher's findings. In theory, this avoids waste in producing things that won't sell, and makes it possible to direct advertising at a carefully selected audience.

In practice, market research often leads companies up the garden path. Consumers are asked what they intend to buy, regardless of whether they have given the matter serious thought, and often at a time when they couldn't care less. Many people, moreover, make fun of researchers by deliberately giving phoney answers. Another problem is that few people know what they really want; they are better at telling questioners what they don't like, and even then their comments may be misleading. A typical example is the general verdict of opinion polls, just before the 1970 General Election, that the Labour Government would be re-elected by a handsome margin. It wasn't.

Market research is a useful tool, as long as it isn't taken too seriously. The scientific jargon used by researchers is impressive enough. The results, as a rule, are less so.

## MATURITY
Nothing to do with growing up; it means the date on which a loan is due to be repaid, or a life insurance policy becomes payable. It may 'mature' in five years' time, or have five years to 'maturity'. In this sense, it's like a good wine – except that loans rarely get any better with time.

## MEDIA GROUP HEAD
One of the countless titles which advertising men bestow upon themselves to impress us with their importance. 'Media' means newspapers, magazines, television, cinema, posters – anything which provides a platform for the adman's talents. A Group means more than one account. Head can mean anything an adman wants it to mean, but generally signifies that he's in charge of something. Taken together, the three words certainly look more impressive than, say, 'executive in charge of baked beans accounts'.

Other titles you may come across include Account Executive (the fellow who is supposed to look after your interests, but somehow never seems to be around when you want him); Assistant Account Executive (a trainee who does all the work); Copywriter (usually a frustrated novelist who has settled for writing one-line slogans because it's better paid) and Art Director (the chap who decides what kind of pictures should go with the slogans).

There is no good reason why an aspiring millionaire should know any of these titles – except that it *could* save him time and money.

## MEMORANDUM

Pieces of paper in various colours (green, yellow, and white are British favourites) on which thoughts are allegedly summarized. Academic economists are reputed to write the longest memos, but civil servants are not far behind. It's the tornado of paper whirling through the corridors of power that holds the government together; the Ministry of Public Building and Works alone uses more than 100 million sheets of paper and 15 million envelopes a year.

Memo-writing, as the Civil and Public Service Association has pointed out, is an art. A good memo is a joy to behold. The brilliant colours of the paper, the neatly typed rows of scintillating Whitehall prose, the tiny, elegant initials of the author – these are things which cannot possibly be replaced by a soulless phone call. It is not only their appearance which makes memos so important. They are also an invaluable substitute for decisions. Decision taking is always an unpleasant business, liable to upset colleagues and friends. It's much nicer just to write a memo. 'Should we', you ask, 'do something about sludge?' The memo is fed into the pipeline, passes through the trays of twenty grateful colleagues, and with a little luck ends up on the Minister's red box. This gives the Minister a chance to write a memo to the Permanent Secretary, who in turn will pass the memo – duly initialed – back along the line. In industry the process may be a little faster, but is essentially the same.

One of the many useful functions of the memo is to show what a clever chap you are. Assume, for example, that someone in your office has a really good idea. If you're quick, you can get it down on paper before he does. By the time he gets back to his desk, your memo is already on its way to the top. If he's foolish enough to write a memo of his own, it will simply look as if he has shamelessly stolen the idea from you. Similarly, a slip by one of your rivals can be brought to the attention of the department chief by a solicitous memo offering help. 'I'm sorry to hear', you tell your rival, 'that your decision has produced such unfortunate results. Do let me know if I can do anything to get you out of this mess.' Twenty copies, circulated to heads of departments, should do a most gratifying amount of damage.

## MERCHANT BANKS

Officially, one of the small group of banks who are 'acceptance houses', meaning they have the Bank of England's backing to guarantee payment by one firm to another. They are 'merchant' banks because most of them were merchants before they became bankers. They traded in all sorts of commodities, and later found it more profitable to leave the actual trading to others and to deal in credit instead of goods. Most of the founders of the best-known merchant banks are descendants of seventeenth-century traders on the Continent: the Rothschilds came from Frankfurt, the Barings from Bremen, the Warburgs and Schroders from Hamburg, the Brandts from St Petersburg, the Lazards from Alsace. Morgan Grenfell was founded in 1838 by an American called George Peabody, whose family came from St Albans in Hertfordshire.

The 'acceptance business' is less important than it used to be, because so many companies today are bigger than the merchant banks and can afford to finance themselves. But most of the merchant banks are still privately owned, and they are deeply involved in industry. They help small firms to raise finance, and bring like-minded companies together in corporate marriage. They act on behalf of individual companies in takeover fights, and frequently get themselves appointed to company boards. Some industrialists think they are troublemakers. Joe Hyman, for example, once told me that 'they think up deals and egg you on, so they can make a fat profit'.

The merchant banks themselves claim they are a uniquely British institutions. They correspond, roughly, to the American investment bank or the French *banque d'affaires*, but they have something extra: their extraordinarily wide range of contacts makes them, perhaps, the most influential sector of one of the most influential financial centres in the world. It's one reason why I would advise any young man with financial acumen to get himself a job

123

with a merchant bank if he can: experience suggests that it is the quickest way to the top of the business tree. A company, large or small, seeing either new capital or better relations with a rival will, sooner or later, seek the advice of a merchant bank. The advice is readily given, in return for a fee, but as a rule both sides insist on continued 'surveillance'. It means that someone at the bank will step straight into a directorship. It beats working!

## MICRO-ECONOMICS
One of the branches of economics; as its name implies, it is concerned with detail. Economists specializing in this area are chiefly concerned with the economic behaviour of individuals and well-defined small groups of individuals. Prices play a major role in micro-economic theories. People, unfortunately, have developed an annoying habit of behaving irrationally and forecasts based on theories often turn out to be rather wide of the mark. To an academic economist, of course, this is of no great consequence – his satisfaction is largely derived from proving points on paper. Some experts, however, think that *macro-economics* is more useful. Macro means taking a broader view; this branch is concerned with general behaviour, and the economy as a whole.

## MILLION
Unit of currency in daily use among government officials charged with the task of deciding how to spend our money. Also used increasingly by large corporations, whose leaders do not like to be bothered with lesser sums. Individuals who possess at least one of these units are known as millionaires, but the word means different things in different countries. It's much easier, for example, to become a dollar millionaire than a sterling millionaire – and in Italy, a million lire is less than £700. Journalists use the label fairly indiscriminately, to add glamour to a story that might otherwise be very dull. Few people actually have a million in the bank; real millionaires tend to be shrewd investors. They may be *worth* a million pounds, but paper values can be misleading. Share prices can go down, as well as up, and fortunes sometimes take a nose-dive overnight. If the money is tied up in plant and equipment, a

millionaire may actually find himself hard up. However good these assets may look in the balance sheet, they only mean something if they produce a reasonable profit – and if it's possible to find a buyer for them at any given point. Because of this – plus the natural tendency for most people to exaggerate their personal wealth – it pays to be sceptical when you read that someone is a millionaire.

## MIXED ECONOMY

One in which some parts of productive industry are owned privately and some publicly. Britain has a mixed economy; basic industries like steel, coal and power are nationalized and subject to government direction, whilst most of our manufacturing industry is in private hands. It complicates economic management and means that the government has much less power than it likes to pretend. Unions tend to have a good deal of say over the level of wages, and it is industry – not Whitehall – which fixes prices and decides on the level of investment in new plant and equipment. Planning and forecasting are both more difficult than they would be if we had a 'controlled' economy.

## MOBILITY

The degree to which labour and capital is willing and able to move elsewhere. Movement of capital is often impeded by exchange controls (see page 79). Movement of labour is extensive, especially among the young, who are less weighed down by commitments. People may switch from one region to another, if a better job is available there, or from one industry to another, if the latter seems to offer better prospects. The process is, of course, made easier if employers are willing to help with housing and the like. Mobility is an important factor in economic management; it is clearly wasteful if one part of the country has a high rate of unemployment, and another a serious shortage of labour.

Many people, of course, also seek jobs abroad. Canada and Australia have always been popular, but Britain's entry into the Common Market could mean considerable movement between Britain and the Continent. The Common Market rules provide for free interchange of labour, and this has already been achieved inside the Community. Work permits have gone, and things have been made much easier for workers who move across Common Market borders. There is an international vacancy clearing system, which tells workers where the most jobs are. The European worker doesn't need to have a job in another market country before he moves there: he simply packs his bags and joins the queue. Once he has moved, he can take advantage of the complex system that the Community has devised to ensure that the migrant worker who pays social security contributions while he is abroad accumulates the same benefits as his foreign workmates. The migrant worker has health insurance in the country where he works; if his family stays at home and needs medical treatment while he is away, the country in which he is working will pay the cost. If he becomes unemployed he will, from 1973, be able to draw unemployment benefit paid by the country where he has been working, even if he goes abroad again to look for a job in another country. Family allowances are paid to the workers' family – even if they stay at home – by the country where he is working at the normal rate.

Continental workers, of course, will have the same rights to seek jobs in Britain. It could, over the years, produce a significant change in social habits – more inter-marriage, new holiday and retirement areas, and the creation of a new, genuine breed of 'Europeans'. But there are snags, too. Mobility is more difficult for people seeking jobs in public services, and for the professional classes. Qualifications such as degrees and diplomas still mean very different things in different countries.

## MODEL

A theoretical construction designed to represent, as far as possible, what happens in real life. Economists have been known to build tangible models (one made a model of the price system using a large water tank and floats) but usually they are content with paperwork. Most would prefer to make controlled experiments with actual people, but since this is difficult to arrange they make do with assembling various known influences and relationships and constructing an edifice which, they hope, comes close to reality. The Treasury, for example, uses a macro-economic model in preparing the annual budget to estimate its probable effects on economic performance. Model building is a fascinating exercise, and many economists take enormous pleasure in it. But models which incorporate expectations (as opposed to those which are purely mechanical) often fail because people don't behave the way they are supposed to. Politicians and trade union leaders, in particular, are inclined to defy logic.

## MONETARY POLICY

The use, by governments, of various methods to influence the economy through interest rates, control of banking and hire–purchase credit, and regulation of foreign money coming in and out of the country. It is one of the two main weapons in the hands of a government. The other is 'fiscal policy', meaning the management of an economy through variations in taxes and the like. Some governments place more reliance on monetary policy than others. In difficult times, and particularly when one's currency is under pressure, there is a tendency to make use of a severe credit squeeze. One political merit is that it is, as a rule, less unpopular than straightforward increases in taxation or a wage freeze. But there is a good deal of argument, among experts, about the effectiveness of monetary policy in economic management. Most are agreed that it is wrong to place too much reliance on this side alone: ideally, it should be used in conjunction with other measures. But, of course, it's the politicians who have the last word. (See MONEY SUPPLY.)

## MONEY

A substance known in America as 'the poor man's credit card' and in Russia as 'the element that makes stupidity shine'. In Britain, we like to pretend that we are not very interested in money, but for all that we talk an awful lot about it.

Nowhere else – no, not even in America – do newspapers devote so much space to money affairs. And nowhere else do people get quite so involved in arguments over how much one should pay the head of state, elected leaders, business executives, doctors, and dustmen.

We remain largely indifferent when it's a matter of how much to

spend on fighter planes, troops, foreign aid, and grants and subsidies, even if the amounts involved run into hundreds of millions.
Public money is a concept which, to most of us, has little meaning.
But let an individual – or a group of individuals – try to procure a
little extra and we all feel qualified, indeed compelled, to pass in-
stant judgment.

There is a basic shabbiness about all our arguments over money:
a joyless, suspicious, resentful mood which makes Britain look
disturbingly petty. The Americans and Germans worship success;
we give the impression that we despise it.

The chief reason is, of course, that we've had appallingly little
economic growth since the end of the last war. A vigorous, expan-
sionist climate makes it possible for everyone to progress. We don't
mind seeing others do well if we're doing nicely ourselves. Retrench-
ment, on the other hand, invariably produces ill-feeling.

Not surprisingly, no one ever admits that his complaints are
inspired by envy. We like to claim that our objections have a more
noble base. So we talk about morality.

Some of the loudest protests against the alleged sinfulness of
trying to acquire money come from those who already have more
than an adequate amount of it. People are bitterly opposed on what
they claim are moral grounds to pay claims, strikes, betting, welfare
benefits, and others ways of making what appears to them a wholly
unjustified attempt to encroach on their territory. The moral
grounds, invariably, consist of the assertion that the 'country is in a
mess' – which, in one form or another, it always is. (If it isn't the
balance of payments, it's inflation, and if it isn't inflation, it's unemployment.) Trade unions who want more money are 'letting
Britain down'.

At the other end of what remains of our class structure, militant
trade unionists and left-wing MPs insist that profits, dividends,
inherited wealth, money made on stocks and shares, large houses
and even business expenses are fundamentally immoral.

Somewhere in the middle are the people who have neither wealth
nor the trade unions' bargaining power. They are the teachers, doctors, parsons and judges who resent the fact that status should nowadays be judged by a yardstick which clearly puts them in second or

third place. Unable to keep up, they condemn 'materialism' and sing the praises of poverty. 'Money doesn't buy happiness,' they intone. And, of course, 'money is the root of all evil'.

All sections seem agreed on at least one thing: even worse than trying to make money is to enjoy spending it. To enjoy money is considered vulgar and depraved; to enjoy it publicly is a sin.

Perhaps this is the real 'English disease'? (See CREDIT CARD.)

## MONEY SUPPLY
A term which, surprisingly, did not become fashionable until the late 1960s. Definitions vary, but basically the concept is meant to cover bank deposits plus notes and coins in the hands of the public.

What makes it really interesting is the argument, which began in the late 1960s, between two camps of experts. On the one side, there are those who believe in the superiority of fiscal policy (use of taxes and the like) and of interest rates in economic management. On the other, there are those who argue that both have been much over-rated, and that it's no less important to concern oneself with the quantity of money which is around at any given point of time. The latter camp, of which Professor Milton Friedman of Chicago has long been the acknowledged leader, has been much helped by the fact that heavy reliance on fiscal policy and interest rates has not, in recent years, produced the results which were hoped for and confidently expected. The Friedman case, basically, is that money supply can and should be controlled, that it has a bigger effect on total expenditure than tax changes, and that the authorities should aim at a fixed and steady growth in the quantity of money – say 5% a year – and not try to chop and change in accordance with their reading of the economic barometer.

The US Treasury, the British Treasury and Bank of England, the Bank of France and other authorities have all accepted that the Professor has a valid point and, in practice, much more attention is now paid to it. But everyone, including Friedman himself, is aware that it is not, by itself, a panacea. 'We are', warns Friedman, 'in danger of assigning to monetary policy a larger role than it can perform, in danger of asking it to accomplish tasks that it cannot achieve, and, as a result, in danger of preventing it from making the

E

contribution that it is capable of making. A steady rate of monetary growth at a moderate level can provide a framework under which you can have little inflation and much growth. It will not produce perfect stability, it will not produce heaven on earth. It will make an important contribution to a stable economic society.'

If nothing else, Friedman's argument has led to a general awareness that fiscal policy and changes in money supply should reinforce each other and not pull in opposite direction. It may strike you as obvious – but that certainly is not how it appeared to officialdom in earlier years. (See also MONETARY POLICY.)

## MOONLIGHTING

Having a second full- or part-time job. Skilled workers like carpenters, painters, and plumbers are particularly fond of moonlighting, but the practice is also growing among white-collar professions like accountancy. In America, not long ago, a major university discovered that one of their professors also held down a lectureship at a college several hundred miles away. He commuted between the two. The professor lost his job, partly because he had concealed his moonlighting activities and partly because the university felt that any man in a responsible position can only do one thing satisfactorily at a time. Most industrial employers share that view. One can usually spot a moonlighter by his tendency to yawn or fall asleep at his main job. His biggest enemy, though, is not his employer (one can always get another one) but the tax collector. Concealing earnings from taxmen is a risky business.

## MULTI-NATIONALS

One of the business catch-phrases of the seventies, often said to be 'the most exciting' development in modern industry. Based on the view that this is the age of the large corporation, transcending old-fashioned national boundaries. Common Market enthusiasts foresee the creation of a great many large and efficient European companies 'capable of carrying out a global economic strategy'. This could be achieved by, for example, promoting a merger between British, French, and German electronics companies. Such a giant, internationally owned and controlled, could unify its research and development and use the EEC as a base for 'invading' world markets. It would gain, the economies of scale. One argument in favour is the growing power of American giants like General Motors and IBM, who already have subsidiaries in many different countries.

The concept sounds excitingly positive, and is backed by the actual experience of existing international corporations like Royal Dutch Shell and Unilever. But there are several important obstacles, notably the fact that Europe does not yet have a unified company law. And a growing number of politicians and economists are worried about the effect which the concentration of industrial power is having on the consumer. Size is no guarantee of efficiency: on the contrary, experience over the past decade suggests that it often leads to exactly the opposite. And, of course, less competition reduces choice and frequently means higher prices. The urge to merge exists, and is perhaps stronger now throughout Europe than it has ever been before. Every industrialist is aware of it; so is almost every trade union executive. But at the same time, there is more scepticism about the likely outcome. This is all to the good. The giant corporation, as I argued in my book *Merger Mania* (Constable, 1970) is not necessarily the best solution to the problems of the seventies. Multi-nationals are here to stay, but there will be plenty of cause for regret if the enthusiasm is overdone.

## NAFTA
Short for North Atlantic Free Trade Area, a scheme proposed in the sixties as an alternative to British membership of the Common Market. The idea was that Britain and the United States should join together in a separate club. NAFTA had several prominent supporters on both sides of the Atlantic, but failed to make much impact where it counts – at the top.

Lyndon Johnson poured cold water on the scheme when it was suggested to him in 1967. He was not interested in forming closer ties with us. Nor was Congress. The proposal was revised when Richard Nixon became president, but it soon transpired that he was no more enthusiastic. Britain's place, he let it be known, was in the Common Market.

# NATIONAL DEBT

Frequently, and quite wrongly, said to be the amount a country owes to other countries. It is, in fact, largely the total of what successive governments have borrowed from us – the public. The major part of Britain's national debt represents borrowing to finance Government expenditure in the two world wars.

Citizens who put up the money were given Government bonds in exchange. The best known of these bonds is War Loan $3\frac{1}{2}\%$, quoted on the Stock Exchange, but there are many others. Bonds which have no fixed repayment date, like War Loan, are known as 'funded debt' – i.e. the debt has become permanent. Other borrowing, including Treasury bills, national savings certificates, and premium bonds, is called 'unfunded debt' and has to be repaid in due course. This can be done either by raising the necessary money through taxation or, more probably, through issuing new Government 'paper' with a different repayment date. Both in theory and in practice, the national debt can go on forever.

Occasionally, voices are raised in protest. In America, for example, the late President Eisenhower once said that 'in effect we are stealing from our grandchildren in order to satisfy our desires of today'. But economists pour scorn on that kind of thinking: all we are doing, they maintain, is to leave to posterity a contractual transfer and re-shuffling of the national income of the time. In short, the word 'debt' has acquired a new, more sophisticated (or, if you prefer, cynical) meaning. You borrow without ever intending to repay; your sons can also arrange things in such a way that the question of actual repayment does not arise.

There are, as you might expect, snags in such a philosophy. The first and most obvious is that governments find it much easier to borrow whatever they like, to finance whatever mad project may take their fancy (including wars). The second is that, although you can 'roll over' the repayment of capital, you cannot avoid paying interest. In the case of undated stocks like War Loan, of course, this can be conveniently small, but future generations of investors are unlikely to show enthusiasm for stocks which yield an insignificant return. The cost of 'servicing' the national debt is, therefore, likely to grow rather than diminish. And if some of the bonds are bought by people living in other countries, the interest paid on them is bound to be a burden on the balance of payments. As long as the money raised in this way is invested in projects which show a return, such as the construction of a new dam or a steel plant, this does not really matter. After all, private enterprise does not have a monopoly on worthwhile ventures. But if the Government has nothing to show for its expenditure, the debt is indeed a charge on future generations – though much less, in pure financial terms, than is generally believed. The two World Wars are the most obvious examples. They did not produce the kind of return that looks good on a balance sheet; the question you have to ask yourself is whether they were worth it in other ways. (See also GILT-EDGED.)

## NATIONALIZED INDUSTRIES

Industries owned by the public – which means you and I. In practice, we have no claim on them of any kind. Indeed we may lose by the arrangement, because their monopoly power allows them to fix whatever level of prices is considered appropriate. Nationalization is essentially a socialist concept, based on the argument that essential services (or the 'commanding heights') should be in the hands of the community or its workers – meaning the Government. In Britain, electricity, steel, power, coal, railways, the principal airlines and even the Bank of England are all owned and controlled by the State.

Perhaps the most persuasive argument in favour of nationalization is that it helps not only to safeguard public services (nationalized industries can't go bust) but can also be used to ensure a certain amount of social justice. It is, for example, much easier for a government to keep down railway fares by agreeing to make good any losses, than it would be if the railway system were still in private hands. It can also stimulate the economy by promoting new capital investment in plant and machinery. Not least, nationalization can be used to preserve military security: priorities can be clearly laid down, and there is less risk of a conflict of interests.

The British Labour Party has, nevertheless, lost much of its former enthusiasm for the process. This is partly because voters turned against the idea of extending it much beyond the basic services, and partly because the party's leaders found alternative ways of controlling the 'commanding heights'. One was to make more effective use of the Government's immense purchasing power: firms were told that, unless they did this or that, they would no longer get vast and lucrative government contracts. Another was to lay down guidelines – and, for a time, actual laws – governing prices and incomes. These and other methods, such as the sponsoring of mergers and industrial reorganization, have often been called 'back-door nationalization'.

## NEAR-CASH

Assets which can be quickly turned into cash, such as Treasury Bills or other easily marketable securities. A business often finds itself with sizeable amounts of money which are not immediately needed. The directors may decide to leave it on current account with the company's bank, but it's often more advantageous to put it on short-term deposit, buy Treasury Bills, lend it to a reputable borrower, or find some other profitable employment. The important thing is that it should be safe and withdrawable at short notice – usually seven days.

## NEDDY

National Economic Development Council (NEDC), a body created by the Conservatives in 1962 to bring economists, businessmen, trade union leaders and ministers together in a common endeavour to find out where we have been, and where we're going. As a party the Tories are naturally less enthusiastic planners than the Socialists, but it was thought that Neddy would help to expand the economy by getting industry to set targets for economic growth, and persuading companies to commit themselves for years ahead. The idea was really stolen from the French, whose *Commissariat au Plan* had been in operation for some time past. The Labour Party, which took over in 1964, continued with the experiment. As a talking shop, Neddy has proved of some value, but the results of its deliberations have, on the whole, fallen well short of expectations. This is partly because planning, as such, has met with growing scepticism.

Not content with Neddy, Mr Wilson's government set up a Department of Economic Affairs (now abolished) and devised a

National Plan. The Plan was proclaimed (by Harold Wilson), as 'a breakthrough in the whole history of economic government by consent and consensus' and welcomed in the House of Commons by all parties. It laid down various objectives, including a 4% annual rate of growth. Alas, the sterling crisis of 1966 got in the way and the great plan was formally buried. The Government's precious targets were swept aside by an orthodox deflationary package, hurriedly introduced to convince the international financial community that Britain could hold the exchange rate at $2.80 to the pound. Neddy still exists and there are all kinds of economic blueprints, but both planners and industrialists have become much more cautious.

In addition to Neddy, the Tories also created the so-called 'Little Neddies' – councils for individual industries, designed to bridge the gap between Whitehall and industry. They were neither executive nor negotiating bodies; their main job was to gather information about a particular industry's activities, spotlight individual problems, promote understanding and use of modern management techniques, and help to eliminate or at least reduce restrictive practices. Labour carried on with them – but, as with Neddy, found itself disappointed with the results.

## NEW

A perfectly ordinary word, but one which qualifies for inclusion because it's a veteran of a thousand expert campaigns. Advertising men, politicians, economists, and of course journalists use it constantly – often to describe something which is no more new than New York or New Orleans. Presidents and prime ministers like to think that everything they do is 'new'. What they really mean, of course, is that it's different – and not necessarily better. Mr Edward Heath, Britain's Premier, has the proud distinction of using 'new' more often in a single speech than anyone else. At the 1971 Tory Party Conference, he said 'new' no less than eighteen times in under an hour. We were, he declared, living in a new world, a world where America and Russia are looking for a new place to stand, where the new voices of each nation are being heard, where new patterns of power are being established, where countries are being forced to look for new ideas and new markets. And guess what he thought we should do about it? Right first time. We had to 'walk out into the light to find a new place. A new Britain in a New World'.

## NUMBERED ACCOUNT

A device invented by the Swiss to attract bank deposits. A client is known by a number instead of his name: his real identity is, as a rule, known only to two or three top officers of each bank. He seldom gets any interest on his money, and may actually be asked to pay a modest sum for the privilege of running the account. Banks in Canada, the Lebanon and elsewhere offer much the same facility, but no one else has developed it to quite the same extent. Swiss banking law relating to secrecy was passed in 1934, at a time when a lot of Jewish money was beginning to leave Germany and Nazi agents were trying to discover where it was going. Swiss bankers never fail to point this out when they are attacked for providing what, in effect, amounts to an open invitation to dodge taxes.

Most numbered accounts are used by businessmen as a means of protecting themselves against the curiosity of their own governments. In Britain and America, the tax authorities can usually prise information about a customer's finances out of his bank. If all else fails, they can get an injunction ordering the bank to disclose. Not so in Switzerland: the Swiss, taking a relatively mild view of income tax evasion, have laid down that banks are under no obligation to tell the authorities anything about their customers' accounts. Italian businessmen, who appreciate this more than most, often enter Switzerland with suitcases full of banknotes and open numbered accounts on the spot.

Besides the obvious financial advantages they offer, numbered accounts are also considered an important status symbol. If you want to open one, you simply walk into one of the banks in Zürich or Geneva, and make your intention known. The official in charge will probably try to convince you that a numbered account is not really needed, since the Swiss banking secrecy laws pertain to all accounts and, further, a numbered account may be against your country's laws. If you insist, and your credentials are in order, your wish will probably be granted. But be sure of one thing: there's no guarantee of secrecy if the prospective client has robbed a bank (which, understandably, is considered a most dreadful thing to do) or is known to have taken part in criminal fraud. This became apparent when the question of fraud was raised in the Clifford Irving case: the bank concerned readily agreed to cooperate with American and Swiss investigators.

## OECD

An organization founded in 1961 to succeed the OECD, which was founded much earlier to work with the ECA to implement the ERP. All right, you are no wiser. I have already had my say on the initials cult (see SPIT) so I won't keep you in suspense: OECD stands for Organization for Economic Cooperation and Development, which I concede is quite a mouthful. It's origins go back to the post-war Marshall Plan, or European Recovery Programme (ERP) and it is supposed to be a 'co-ordinating body for economic co-operation in Europe'. In short, a talking shop.

## OLD LADY OF THREADNEEDLE STREET

Affectionate nickname for the Bank of England. According to the Bank itself, its origin was a cartoon by James Gilray, published during the Napoleonic wars. It showed William Pitt the Younger, then Prime Minister and Chancellor of the Exchequer, attempting to get possession of the bank's gold from an elderly lady seated on a locked chest. The title 'Political Ravishment, or the Old Lady of Threadneedle Street in danger' is thought to have come from Sheridan, the dramatist, who earlier in the year had spoken of the Bank in the House of Commons as 'an elderly lady in the City of great credit and long standing'.

## OPEN MARKET OPERATIONS

One of the methods used by central banks, such as the Bank of England and the Federal Reserve, to regulate the volume of credit and influence rates. If a central bank wants to increase the amount of money in circulation, it goes into the market and buys up Government bonds and Treasury Bills. The money it spends will increase

E*

the balances of the clearing banks (who are generally the main sellers) and this will enable them to lend even more to the public. If, on the other hand, it feels the need for some restraint, it goes in for large-scale selling of securities. This mops up money, the banks reduce their advances to customers, and the public cuts back spending. Open market operations can be quite effective, but are only part of the armoury available to economic managers: they're no miracle cure for real financial ills.

## OPM

Shorthand for 'Other People's Money'. It's the surest way to acquire wealth. The Hilton Hotel chain was built up on credit, and there are countless other examples of people who have made fortunes with OPM. 'Show me a millionaire', William Nickerson has been quoted as saying, 'and I will show you invariably a heavy borrower.'

One favourite post-war trick has been to make a share-exchange offer for a company rich in property assets, and to turn these into cash immediately after acquiring control. This is how financier Charles Clore got the Sears shoe chain for nothing. He offered shareholders the lure of quick gain by making a bid which valued the shares at considerably more than the current market level. The Board of Directors defended itself in vain. He secured 75% acceptances, and at once started to sell hundreds of freehold shops to financial institutions, who were always on the lookout for ways of employing their huge incomes. They paid for the shops in cash – and promptly leased them back to him. Clore got, in effect, control of properties worth more than £8 million. It laid the foundation for a considerable trading empire and, inevitably, a number of other eye-catching takeover deals.

## OPTIONS

A speculative device which looks attractive on paper, and often is in practice. There are three types of options: a 'call' option, a 'put' option, and a 'double' option. A 'call' option is the most popular; paid to a broker, it gives you the right to buy a given share at the existing price at any time over the following three months. In short, if you have reason to think that a share will go up, you can get hold of it without actually laying out a lot of money. You simply pay the price of the option – which may be as little as three new pence, or as much as fifty new pence a share. (The rates for leading stocks are quoted each day in *The Financial Times*.) If you've guessed wrong, your loss is limited to that amount. If you've made a good choice, you have secured a profit at a known risk. Some people think that options are the greatest thing that ever happened to the Stock Exchange. Perhaps so – but remember that, to make the deal worth-while, the market price of the shares has to show quite a substantial rise.

A 'put' option works in reverse; it gives you the right to sell at the existing price at any time over the following three months; of course your broker has to buy them for you to sell them, and the cost re-flects the risk he takes. It's something for pessimists – or, as they like to think, realists. A 'double' option allows you to have it both ways – but the price of indecision is double that of either the 'call' or the 'put'.

No, I don't know why they're called put and call. It's one of those things which is a mystery even to the expert.

## OTHER THINGS BEING EQUAL
One of the old-time greats in economics; you can generally tell whether a man is an economist by the number of times he uses this particular phrase. It's a useful way of dismissing qualifications at the start of an argument. 'Other things being equal', you say, 'the following should happen.' There's only one snag; other things are usually *not* equal.

## OVERHEADS
Costs which are not directly attributable to any particular item you produce. Head office expenses are the most obvious example, but it can be almost anything – from the money you have paid for a machine, truck or typewriter to your secretary. Because they are so hard to pin down, they have a tendency to run away with themselves, especially in good times. (See COST-CUTTING.)

## PAPER PROFITS

One of the more deceptive things in business. You may have bought a share which is doing well, or backed a restaurateur who seems to be enjoying a great success. On paper, you show a healthy profit. But there's an old Stock Exchange maxim which says, quite reasonably, that paper profits don't mean a thing until you take them. The great Rothschild once said, when asked how he made his fortune, that he had done it by 'always selling too soon'. It may sound glib, and in a way it is. Rothschild didn't have to worry about a capital gains tax. But it's certainly a point worth bearing in mind. Paper profits are fine as long as there is little likelihood that they will vanish. Unfortunately, they often do.

## PAR VALUE

The nominal value of shares or investments. Shares may be issued in units of 10p, 20p, 50p, or 100p, and dividends are expressed as a percentage of these values. But it doesn't mean the shares are worth that amount at any given moment. Their market value is only loosely linked to the par value: it very much depends on what investors are prepared to pay for a particular stock. They usually prefer to back the future rather than the past, and they tend to take account of the capital employed in the business rather than the nominal value of the issued shares. The same applies to certain other investments, but not to money deposited with a bank or building society: £100 will keep its par value (if not its purchasing power) for as long as the money remains with them.

## PARTNERSHIP

Two or more people involved in the ownership or control of a business. The relationship between them is governed by the agreement they draw up; if there is no written agreement, the Partnership Act of 1890 lays down that all partners are equal as regards profits and losses. The liability of partners is not limited; each one of them is liable to an unlimited extent not only for his own share of the firm's debts but also for the share of the others. For this reason, many people try to avoid this rather extreme kind of relationship. A sleeping partner (one who takes no active part in the running of the

140

business, but has a stake in its profits or losses) may prefer to take advantage of the Limited Partnership Act 1907, which restricts both his rights and his liability. More popular still, though, is the private limited liability company. It is a much less dangerous device, because the shareholder's risk is limited to the amount he has invested in the firm. Businessmen, in particular, usually prefer this to the old-fashioned partnership. It's mainly the professions – medicine, accountancy, and the law – which keep the partnership principle going.

## PATENT
A legal right to make, use, or sell an invention during the period the patent remains in force – usually sixteen years. An International Convention for the Protection of Industrial Property helps to secure patent rights abroad by giving the patent-holder in a member country priority in obtaining similar patents in another country. The United States, the Soviet Union, Britain and other European countries all belong to it.

Before an invention will be patented it must be proved to contain an element of novelty. And it won't be granted if the invention, or its use, is contrary to law or morality, or if it consists of foodstuffs or medicine with no other properties than the ingredients are already known to contain. This clearly involves some interesting questions of judgment. How 'novel' does an idea have to be to qualify? And how does one decide, in these permissive days, how far it may be 'contrary to morality'? No, it's no good asking the authorities; they will not give either advice or financial assistance.

## PATERNALISM
A system which claims to look after people, but which all too often means a twentieth-century form of slavery. Specially prominent in Japan. On paper, Japanese paternalism sounds very noble. There is an unwritten law that says you don't ever fire anyone. Big firms recruit young men straight from school or college and, as a rule, employ them 'for life'. Employers tend to talk of 'adopting workers into the family', and people who change jobs two or three times in the course of their lives risk being described as 'unstable characters'.

Luring workers away from other companies is considered bad form. If a company runs into a bad patch, it reduces working hours and bonuses – but keeps its men. If they are inefficient, or make several bad mistakes, they are demoted rather than sacked. Fringe benefits are impressive.

On close inspection one begins to see a few snags. The benefits merely help to make up for comparatively low wages. And they tie a man down completely – which means, as a rule, that he is at the mercy of his bosses. They will expect him to put his job above all else, even to the point of working long hours overtime without reward, giving up weekends, and foregoing annual holidays. If he cannot get on with his immediate superior, life can be hell. In theory he can move, but he cannot take his accumulated benefits with him and he may be judged unreliable. So he usually stays. His career is blueprinted at the start, and seniority usually counts for more in determining salary increases and promotion than ability. At fifty-five, the company will retire him with a modest lump sum and he will get a social security pension which is seldom big enough to keep him in the life style to which he has grown accustomed. Paternalism has contributed greatly to Japan's economic success, but many young Japanese intensely dislike it. They have already forced some changes, and more are likely to come.

## PEACE SCARE
Headline sometimes used by journalists to frighten American businessmen. When the Vietnam peace talks started in Paris, for example, a well-known business magazine announced: 'Real threat of peace in Vietnam.'

Underlying this is the widely-held belief that economic prosperity is difficult, if not impossible, to achieve without heavy defence spending. If you look at America's economic history since World War II, you will see that Korea and Vietnam both produced boom periods. And not only, one hastens to add, for the United States. Dozens of other countries had their economies boosted by Washington's massive war expenditure. Thailand, South Korea, the Philippines, Japan, Malaysia, and Europe all benefited enormously from America's faith in military strength.

The Paris peace talks, on the other hand, were followed by a period of widespread economic decline. In the US itself, unemployment soared to disturbing levels. Elsewhere, governments struggled to make ends meet.

Defence spending accounts for nearly 10% of America's gross national product. Whole industries are geared to war. Defence business is like no other: there is only one major customer for your output, salesmanship is not put to the test in the open market, and if you know of any engineer who can convert a shipyard into a plant making toasters or anti-pollution devices – well, a lot of industrialists would like to hear from you.

Given our modern, allegedly sophisticated economic management techniques, it seems absurd that peace – or the prospect of it – should cause any problems. It is indeed possible to find effective alternative ways of keeping an economy in a healthy state. The Administration certainly is not short of complex plans. But there is no doubt that 'peace scares' still make some people nervous. In the long run peace must be bullish; in the short run it tends to produce changes which are bound to hurt someone, somewhere.

## PERFECT COMPETITION
One of the many things which economists love to talk about, but which do not actually exist. It's really an analytical 'model' of the pure form that a market would take. It involves such requirements as (1) a lot of sellers of an identical product so that none could influence the market; (2) everybody knows exactly what goes on in this and other markets; (3) every producer's product is identical; (4) no one is big enough to dominate the market; (5) there are no barriers to the movement of capital or workers. Need one say more? It's pure Utopia.

## PERFORMANCE CONTRACT
An arrangement under which payment for a job is based on measured results for a specified task. The penalties for failure are, as a rule, carefully spelled out. Management consultants, and others offering a service rather than a product, usually work on this sort of basis. It has even been applied to schools; in the United States

particularly, firms specializing in educational systems have been hired for periods of from one to four years. A problem with many performance contracts is accurately measuring progress: it is usually a matter of opinion.

## PHILIPS CURVE

Would you believe that it's a way of measuring the relationship of general changes in prices to economic activity? Well, that's exactly what it is. And yes, it was thought up by a man named Philips.

## PLACING

A word that means exactly what you think it means – as long as you're familiar with the stock market. If a privately owned firm wants to 'go public' (in other words, to allow outside investors in on whatever thing it has managed to get going) it can consider one of several arrangements. The most popular method is an 'offer for sale' – a well-publicized offer of its shares to the general public. Another is an offer for sale by tender – an offer of shares at any price above a certain minimum, with the highest bidders getting the allocation. If these rather bold methods seem inappropriate, either because the company's advisers reckon there won't be much response or the board doesn't want any fuss, the best method may be a placing. It means, as a rule, that a merchant bank and/or stockbroker approaches a list of clients who may be prepared to buy shares at a price satisfactory to both parties. The shares are literally 'placed' with institutions or wealthy individuals.

## PLOUGHING BACK

Putting profits back into the business, instead of spending them or distributing them to shareholders as dividends. The money may be used to finance expansion, or to modernize existing plant. The process is also known as 'self-financing', and is popular with ambitious and fast-growing companies. The ordinary shareholder benefits in the end, because the value of his assets is increased. Some people prefer this kind of company to one which is generous with dividends. This is because they are more interested in capital gain than income (usually for tax reasons). A high rate of profit retention, however, does not always mean faster growth. If a company is badly managed, the money may be lost on risky ventures. Or it may simply lie in the bank, instead of being used on something worthwhile. Take-over bids, fortunately, have acted as a useful spur in these situations. A board of directors which makes a mess of things, or lacks the imagination and courage to make proper use of the shareholders' money, may well find itself the object of unwelcome attention from a more aggressive rival.

## PORTFOLIO

If you own shares in one company, you are a shareholder. If you have shares in two, you are someone who is running a portfolio. Everyone who aspires to real status in the money world should have a portfolio. It makes life interesting, and offers endless opportunities for impressing other people. Supervising one's portfolio is a splendid spare time activity, and an absorbing pastime in retirement. There are so many things you can do with it, switching from one stock to another, 'averaging' by adding to existing stocks by a purchase of shares at a lower price, nagging your broker three times a day, writing to companies to tell them how to run your business, and talking loudly at cocktail and dinner parties about the impact of world events on your investments. If you happen to have a 'go-go' portfolio so much the better; however dull you may be as a person, it gives you an air of daring which few women can resist. 'Go-go' stocks are those which look destined to go places: with luck, the label will also be applied to you.

## PREFERENCE SHARES

The name is both accurate and misleading – preference shares have a prior claim over holders of ordinary shares, both to dividends and repayment of capital if the company goes bust, but they rank *after* debentures and loan stocks. Dividends are usually at a fixed rate, paid twice a year, but some companies also issue participating preference shares which entitle their holders to a limited share of surplus profits, if any. Unlike ordinary stock, preference shares seldom have voting rights and holders tend to miss out on the handsome profits usually made when there is a takeover bid. Dividends,

145

moreover, are paid only out of profits. If these are not earned, shareholders tend to go dividendless, or get only a part of the amount due. Most issues have a form of protection in that the dividends are cumulative; if one year's profits are not enough to pay the fixed rate, the entitlement is carried forward and must be paid out of any future profits.

Preference shares tend to give a higher return than ordinary stocks, and therefore appeal to people who need a good income. But they do not provide a safeguard against inflation, and for this reason are far less popular than 'equities'. (See DEBENTURES and EQUITIES.)

## PRESTIGE-PAY RATIO

What's it worth, in terms of sacrifice in salary, to gain the prestige which will lead to higher things? Every ambitious young businessman, if he has sense, will work out his own prestige-pay ration. Some people settle for the best they can get right at the start, and stay put. They usually reach a certain level, after several years' service, and find they cannot move much beyond it. Others deliberately accept a low rate, and switch jobs even if it means a cut in immediate income, because the job concerned offers the kind of prestige which tends to act as a natural stepping stone. A junior executive post in a well-known, highly successful company may, for example, be more prestigious in the long run than a high executive position in a small, run-of-the-mill firm. I have, on more than one occasion, willingly taken a sizeable cut in salary because I was convinced a different job had more potential. It's a risky game, of course, and should ideally be indulged in before one runs up too many financial commitments. One must be clear, too, what kind of prestige is involved: a bigger title, no matter how good for the ego, doesn't mean much if it does not mean real advancement – both in terms of money and job satisfaction.

## PRICE-EARNINGS RATIO

One of the tools investment analysts use to evaluate a share. It is highly popular in the United States, and was imported into Britain after the Labour Government introduced corporation tax in 1964.

Analysts say it helps to make comparisons with American stocks, and to see how the market rates any given share compared with others in its field. The p/e ratio, as it is commonly known, indicates the number of years which it would take for the share to earn the amount of its cost. It is arrived at by dividing net earnings into the market price per share. A low p/e ratio implies an expected decline in profits; a high ratio usually means that the market thinks well of the company and looks for higher profits and, possibly, an increased dividend.

The p/e ratio is based on reported earnings, and is therefore out of date by the time it is published – sometimes by many months. It gives no indication of how safe a dividend is. Ideally, one should be able to allow for current and likely future profits, but that's difficult. In the circumstances, it's best not to place too much reliance on the p/e ratio: it's just one of the many factors to be taken into account in making up one's mind about a particular investment.

## PRODUCTIVITY

What you can get out of a man – and his machine – within a given period. Anything wider usually comes under the heading of 'efficiency'. The term should not be, but often is, confused with production, which simply means anything which is made, moved, or provided. The productivity of labour is usually measured as output per man per shift, hour, month, or year. In part, this clearly depends on the man himself. Trade union regulations are also a factor: in many cases, productivity is deliberately held down in order to keep more people working on a project than are really necessary. But a no less important factor is the quality of the equipment provided by the employer. The high level of productivity enjoyed for so many years by countries like the United States, Japan and Germany owes a good deal to substantial investment in modern plants and equipment. In Britain, such investment has been notoriously low. Attempts are made, from time to time, to relate wage increases to increases in productivity. In many companies, binding productivity agreements are in force. They usually work best when both management and workers recognize the basic problems and decide to do something about them.

# PROFIT
Usually defined as the difference between a company's income and outgo – an over-simplification which leaves much room for misunderstanding. Workers tend to see it as pure gain, and to equate it with 'profiteering'. (According to an ex-Labour Minister, they even equate it with incest and lechery.) Properly speaking it ought not to be called profit at all, but trading surplus. A company, after all, still has to make allowance for tax, depreciation, loan stock interest and other unavoidable charges – items which, taken together, tend to cut the figure by more than half. Shop stewards, of course, are well aware of this, but it often suits them to use the word 'profit' as a weapon. This is a hangover from the past, and in some ways one cannot perhaps blame them. Labour has been exploited on countless occasions, and still *is* in some cases. But anyone who takes an objective look at the overall picture will readily acknowledge that times have changed. Trade union power, among other things, has seen to that. There certainly is no case for despising the profit *motive*: they have even come to acknowledge its value in the Soviet Union.

The most sensible yardstick, if one wants to see how a company is doing, is the return on capital employed. Add together fixed assets like plant and machinery and net current assets – the difference between the total of items like cash, outstanding debts and work-in-hand and the total of current liabilities like creditors, overdrafts, taxation and dividends. This is the capital employed. Work out how much the profit shown in the accounts comes to as a percentage of the combined figure. If it compares favourably with other companies in the field, it is a sign that the company is well-managed. If you don't want to be bothered with making the calculation yourself, ask an accountant or stockbroker to do it for you. It shows you know the ropes. (See PAPER PROFIT.)

# PROGRESSIVE TAXATION
The principle which has, for many years, guided the British tax system. Proportional taxation means that payment is made in direct proportion to income; rich and poor alike hand over, say, twenty per cent of their earnings. Progressive taxation means that the better-

off not only pay higher absolute amounts, but also a bigger proportion of their income. This happens because parts of it are subject to increasing rates of tax, as in surtax and estate duty. It was brought in to narrow the gap between rich and poor, and socialists still argue that it is a most practical device for redistributing wealth and income. In short, it is an instrument of justice.

Tories tend to argue, on the other hand, that is is an unwarranted form of discrimination against the individual. They maintain that it penalizes not only the rich, but also the middle-class manager who is the chief driving force in the economy. He cannot accumulate capital, and therefore lacks the funds necessary for independent action. 'What', a nineteenth-century critic of progressive taxation asked, 'would we think of a baker or grocer or any merchant who would demand for the same commodity a price varying with the wealth of the purchaser?' Mr Heath's Government accepts that the principle has been carried too far, and is trying to alter the balance. But neither proportional taxation nor regressive taxation (under which taxes take a higher proportion of smaller incomes) is likely to make a spectacular come-back, either in Britain or in America.

## PROPERTY BOND
An extension of the unit trust principle which inflation has made highly popular. A property bond is a direct investment in a property fund, whose assets are regularly revalued by independent surveyors. It represents, therefore, a way of getting an interest in property (which has tended to appreciate faster in value than ordinary shares in an industrial concern) without taking the risks involved in backing an individual property firm. Abbey Property Bond Fund, the biggest in Britain, has its money in top industrial and commercial properties let to tenants like National Westminster Bank, the Post Office, and American Express. It also buys sites and constructs its own buildings in partnership with approved developers. Abbey, like many other funds, was developed by a life assurance company and bondholders are usually offered built-in assurance, at no extra cost.

## PROXY
A person acting in place of another. If you hold voting shares in a

company, but cannot attend a shareholders' meeting, you are entitled to appoint someone else as your 'proxy' – providing you give
the company advance notice. He can vote on your behalf, even
though he may not be a shareholder himself. This explains why,
very often, a controversial proposal may be defeated on a show of
hands, but approved by an overwhelming majority on a poll.
Directors often solicit proxies in the case of, say, takeover bids. So
does the opposition. American financial history, particularly, is full
of colourful 'proxy fights'.

## PUBLIC COMPANY
Any firm whose shares are bought and sold on the Stock Exchange;
most of the big industrial organizations come into this category. A
private company need have only two shareholders but may not have
more than fifty, it must not invite the public to subscribe capital,
and it must restrict the right to transfer shares. The private company, unlike most partnerships, offers the advantage of limited
liability. Some remain private even when they grow to substantial
size, but most businessmen nowadays aim to 'go public' at some
stage in the future. (See PARTNERSHIP.)

## PUBLIC RELATIONS
A profession which, at its worst, gets in the way of understanding
and, at its best, does a great deal to promote it. Journalists love to
knock PR, and most of those who do so eventually end up in it. Bad
public relations men spend all their time devising new letter heads,
taking people to lunch, arranging meetings between busy executives
who have no wish to meet, writing press releases which are meant
more for the eye of the fee-paying chairman than the press, and
organizing receptions at which the only noteworthy happening is
that everyone present gets drunk. Good public relations men tell
their employers the truth, even if it happens to be unpleasant, look
after their 'customers' in the press and elsewhere (internal PR is
often much more important than relations with papers and magazines) and use their knowledge of human nature to produce the
right kind of results. It's a popular myth that public relations is the
same thing as salesmanship: in fact, a good PR man often spends as

much time trying to keep things out of the paper as putting them in. There is considerable merit in silence; as every successful businessman knows. But there's no harm in selling if the product is sound: but if it isn't, not even the best public relations man can hide the fact in the long run.

## PUBLIC SECTOR
That part of the economy which comes within the scope of the government. (By the same token, private sector means everything owned and controlled by individuals, private limited companies, and corporations quoted on the Stock Exchange.)

The Labour Party has always been keen on expanding the public sector, chiefly through nationalization, because it believes in central planning. Industries like electricity, water, coal, steel, and railways were taken into public ownership many years ago. To this one has to add social services like health, education, and housing, and the local authorities. Under Mr Harold Wilson's Labour Government of 1964–70, ministers gradually steered away from outright nationalization – believing that the same effect could be achieved, with less fuss, by making use of the Government's formidable purchasing power, encouraging mergers, providing public finance with 'strings', and using ministerial influence. A scheme for capturing more of the 'commanding heights of the economy' by the creation of new science-based industries never really got off the ground. The Tories believe in free enterprise and have returned some of the 'public sector' to private investors. They are, however, keenly aware that state ownership of key industries makes it easier to reorganize the British economy, and is a useful weapon in the battle against major problems like wage inflation. (See NATIONALIZED INDUSTRIES.)

## PULL
More often called nepotism, or 'undue patronage to one's relations'. Pull can take many forms, but the basic requirement stays essentially the same – you must know the *right* people, right meaning anyone who can help your career. A man is known by his friends and contacts, and in business it is important to have influential friends. Marrying into a family firm is a recognized way of getting

the first push up the business ladder, but takeover bids and mergers have tended to reduce the scope. Young businessmen who try to acquire pull through marriage sometimes find that, soon after the wedding, the firm is taken over by a bigger outfit and family connections actually prove to be a handicap. The modern managers who run large, go-ahead corporations tend to be biased against anyone who seems to owe his job to favouritism. Push is probably more important, today, than pull. Push means being self-confident, or at least appearing to be self-confident, and bringing your talents to the notice of the people who run corporations or lend big money – ideally without, at the same time, offending all one's colleagues.

## PUMP PRIMING
An attempt to revive a depressed economy by injecting more purchasing power by government spending than is collected in the form of taxes or other revenue. This injection requires a Budget deficit – which is why pump priming is also referred to, from time to time, as deficit spending. The government covers its deficit chiefly by borrowing, which it tends to find a lot easier to do than you and I do. The best-known advocate of pump priming was Lord Keynes: if you want Keynesian economics in one sentence, this is it. The basic idea is that, once the economy has been revived by public spending, an upswing in private expenditure will follow. Unemployment will fall, and the government can afford to relax again. The technique is nowadays used fairly frequently, even in conditions which fall well short of what one could call a depression. The main risk is that too much money is pumped into the economy, over too long a period of time. The combined forces of private and public spending may, eventually, produce 'over-heating' and serious inflation. (See KEYNES.)

## PURCHASE TAX
One of the many wartime innovations which wasn't supposed to last, but did. It was introduced during the Churchill administration of the Second World War, as a means of boosting revenue. Purchase tax is an indirect tax (and therefore less obvious than, say, income tax) and is applied to goods and commodities at the wholesale level.

It has proved a most effective way of raising money, and it allows Chancellors to make value judgments: they can single out individual targets, and therefore decide which areas of spending should be encouraged or discouraged. To help with economic management, the Treasury invented the regulator; this is a device for varying purchase tax rates and excise duty at any given time without going through the tiresome business of seeking parliamentary approval.

## PURCHASING AGENT

The company buyer. He's usually responsible for purchasing raw materials, components, spare parts and equipment – right down to the office stationery. A good man can save his firm a lot of money, but all too often the job goes to a pedantic type who loves to prevaricate. He delights in keeping salesmen on the hook ( and in doing so, sometimes loses the opportunity to buy at a favourable price) and he evolves elaborate procedures which make it impossible to buy, say, a typewriter without filling in a long and pointless application, and waiting at least three months for delivery. Some experts think this is because, in most organizations, the purchasing agent has a comparatively low status. He is certainly considered less important than the men who go out and sell. So he goes in for all this horseplay in order to compensate.

An exception to the rule, of course, are companies where intelligent buying is crucial – such as department stores. A top-class buyer will not only be a skilful negotiator, but will frequently be able to point out to suppliers changes in equipment or techniques which could improve the product or the service offered.

## PYRAMIDING

A form of speculation which is possible only when you can buy stocks on margin – meaning that you put some of your own money down as a deposit, and borrow the rest from your broker at a certain rate of interest. Its popularity in the late 1920s was one of the reasons for the Great Crash. At the time, margin requirements were only 10%. So, to begin with, a speculator bought, say, 100 shares of a $50 stock. He paid down $500 and borrowed the rest. The price of the stock duly went up, reaching $75. He now had a handsome paper profit, but did not cash it. Instead, his broker recognized the increased value as collateral for an even bigger loan to buy an extra number of shares. Some people carried this game to extraordinary length, starting with a few hundred dollars and ending with stock literally worth millions. It worked fine when prices were rising, but often proved disastrous when they began to fall and brokers called in margins. The small-time speculator might suddenly find himself faced with the demand: 'Put up $100,000 additional margin or else.' He could not raise that kind of money without selling – and his selling accelerated the decline in price.

## QUALITY OF LIFE, THE
A phrase increasingly popular with countries which have achieved a high rate of economic growth. In Japan, many thoughtful people are appalled by what economic success has done to their surroundings. America's concern with the 'environment' reflects the same kind of feeling. Their experts criticize Britain's apparent lack of drive, but also tend to envy our more leisurely way of life. There is, they say, no real virtue in hard work as such. Some people enjoy it, and no one would wish to spoil their fun. It is right that they should be properly rewarded, and they usually are. But economic achievement, as measured by the balance of payments and the gross national product, is not an end in itself, but a means to an end. And that end, it is acknowledged, ought to include leisure.

If a worker uses his extra pay to buy more leisure, he is not 'wrecking the country' but simply exercising an option which ought to be granted to every civilized person. If he fights to preserve the beauty of the countryside, even though new factories would give him more prosperity, he is not being 'old-fashioned and backward', but rather more sensible than people who have made economic growth their god.

There's a nice little story which I once heard in South Carolina, and which I have always felt ought to make every economist – and businessmen – pause for a few seconds. It is about an African who was seated under a coconut tree resting, when he was addressed by a passing Englishman. 'What', the Englishman asked, 'are you doing for yourself, just idly sitting here? Why don't you get busy and develop your fields, dig mines, and build cities?' 'What for?' the African asked. 'To establish commerce,' the Englishman replied. 'Commerce for what?' 'So you can make lots of money.' 'What good is money?' 'Money will bring you leisure.' 'What will I do with leisure?' 'Then you can rest.' 'But why do all that', the African asked, 'when I'm resting now?'

## QUARTERBACK
Americans see everything in terms of football or baseball – including business. (In Britain, of course, we prefer cricket.) 'Characteristically,' says Harry Levinson, author of *The Exceptional Executive*, 'the American executive has an image of himself as a combination coach, quarterback, linebacker and end. He designs the plays and calls the signals. He evolves strategy and manages tactics. He tackles the competition head-on, or makes brilliant broken-field marketing runs, or throws surprise product passes over the heads of the competition, or punts the economic ball safely out of danger by merger, cost-cutting, or some other emergency device. And he does it every season.'

Any European planning to do business with an American would, clearly, be well advised to familiarize himself with words like 'quarterback' and 'punt'. White House economic strategy, incidentally, is known as a 'game plan'.

## QUEEN'S AWARD TO INDUSTRY
One of many awards which, according to Lord McFadzean, should be regarded as 'a battle honour given to a military unit' – the unit being a company which does well in overseas markets. The Queen's Award was invented by Harold Wilson because, faced with a constant balance of payments crisis, ministers felt compelled to elevate exporting to one of the highest of human virtues. Never mind the arts; the real test of your value to the community was whether you could sell washing machines to Düsseldorf. There were knighthoods galore for Harold's heroes – brave men, imbued with the spirit of Dunkirk, riding to battle in their Rolls-Royces to save us from oblivion.

We have had a good deal less of this tomfoolery under the Tories, but the Queen's Award – entitling the lucky recipient to fly a specially designed flag from his factory chimney – has become a British institution. Among its recent recipients is Cannon Rubber Manufacturers, who won it for a second time because its Babysafe Division 'has been responsible for a dramatic increase in exports of feeding bottles, teats, soothers, and other baby articles to over 100 countries throughout the world'.

Awards, alas, have become a boom business, a drug we take in ever-increasing doses. There is an extraordinary, and seemingly unstoppable, craving for titles, sashes, pennants, honorary degrees, badges, and statuettes. As the craving grows, so does the search for things to honour. Businessmen have merely taken their cue from showbiz. If Hollywood can indulge itself in such a blatantly phoney way, industry feels justified in doing the same. If television can give awards to its technicians, industry feels that it can safely honour its washing machine salesmen. And yes, if newspapers can give gongs to each other, businessmen reckon that they can reasonably demand to take part in the racket. Merit is where you find it. Shareholders, of course, find it in the balance sheet: profits and dividends are their only yardstick. They are right.

## QUOTAS

Any quantitative restriction on trade, but most commonly applied to the limitation of foreign imports. Governments use quotas to protect domestic industries from foreign competition, or to relieve pressure on the balance of payments. Trade between capitalist and communist countries is mostly subject to quotas; they are fixed in direct negotiations between individual countries. Trade within the free world is not, as a rule, restricted in this way. International rules, however, allow a government to resort to quotas if there is a 'serious decline in monetary reserves'. The opportunity is rarely taken, partly because of the very real possibility of retaliation and partly because a large and complex system is needed to issue licences, check abuses, and generally administer a quota system. Both Britain and the United States have preferred to make use of a surcharge – a straight percentage addition to the cost of virtually every import. The trouble with a surcharge is that firms either pass it on to customers, in the form of higher prices, or absorb it in their profit margins in the hope that it will prove temporary – a move which, of course, defeats the whole purpose of the exercise.

## R and D

Shorthand for research and development. Obviously essential in industries in which competition is largely based on technological innovation. Computers is one example; the aircraft industry is another. America's big companies spend much more on R and D than European concerns, and the need to catch up is said to be one of the chief reasons why we need more European mergers. Studies show, however, that the fertility of innovation is not necessarily related to size. Medium-sized and large (rather than largest) firms often do best. There is an element of hit and miss in R and D; only a small share of research results is capable of economic development. Many good ideas have come from individual inventors, rather than corporate teams. The development of Whittle's jet, for example, from an idea to a proven system cost a mere £25,000. But large expenditure greatly increases the chances of finding something worth developing – and of turning it into a marketable product.

## RATIONALIZATION

Measures taken by companies, or enforced by banks or governments, to improve efficiency (profitability) by reducing the number of units of production and concentrating output in the most efficient (profitable) ones. The merger boom of recent years has generally been regarded as an essential part of a much overdue 'rationalization' process. Many people feel, however, that the results have often been of questionable value. (See also TAKEOVER BID and COST-CUTTING.)

## REAL WAGES

Wages adjusted for changes in the level of prices. A lot of people judge their own personal progress strictly in terms of pay. The factory worker thinks he's better off if his wage packet contains £5 more one week; similarly, the office worker thinks he has advanced if he is granted an 'increment'. They leave out of account the fact that, because of price increases, their real wages may not have risen at all. What matters is what the pound will buy. If its purchasing power declines by 10% a year, then one needs the same sort of rise in income simply to stay in the same place. The Labour Government tried to get this across to people when it introduced an incomes policy, but failed to do so in language that everyone could understand. Many trade union leaders said they were simply concerned with ensuring that their own members, at least, would keep pace with the cost of living – and, if possible, get ahead of it. The chief sufferers were old age pensioners and others living on fixed incomes, because their real income showed a persistent and rapid decline.

## RECESSION

A word which politicians love to use against their rivals; to 'engineer a recession' is to let down the British people. In fact, it may mean no more than a modest reduction in economic activity. The cause may be a recession in one or more of our important export markets, such as the United States, or an attempt to 'save' a fixed exchange rate through deflationary measures such as a credit squeeze and higher taxes. Like 'boom' and 'slump', the word has the inestimable merit of fitting neatly into a headline. Economists resent Fleet Street's urge to label everything in this way. A boom, to them, is either a peak in the business cycle (see page 39) or an all-out expansion of business activity which has been organized by the government of the day in order to win the next election. A recession is somewhere in between, and a slump – which tends to follow – can be anything from a noticeable decline in economic activity – accompanied by a sharp rise in unemployment – to a period of sustained misery in which nothing ever seems to go right, and which looks like going on forever.

Before the Second World War, these phases recurred fairly regularly. Post-war economics, however, has succeeded in evening out fluctuations. Ups and downs have been no less frequent, but less pronounced. Politicians still like to scare us by warning that, if we don't watch our step, we shall see a return to the dreaded thirties. But voters have heard this too often to be greatly impressed: there is a general feeling that politicians 'wouldn't dare'. It flatters them;

politicians have much less power to control events, once they are under way, than most people think.

## REDEMPTION

Nothing to do with religion, but simply financial jargon for 'paying back'. Companies and governments don't repay, they redeem. There's no reason, it's just their policy.

## REDEPLOYMENT

One of several euphemisms used to get around the politically explosive word 'unemployment'. Strictly speaking, it means getting people to find other jobs – an exercise also known as a 'shakeout' or 'releasing surplus labour'. The idea is to put them into industries designated by the government of the day; in times of balance of payments trouble, this usually means exporting firms. It sounds good on paper, but it is difficult to apply in practice. If economic activity is low, there may simply not be enough new jobs available. Retraining facilities, too, are generally inadequate to deal with the sudden 'shakeout' of a large number of men. The biggest snag with redeployment is that people have an irritating habit of behaving like human beings. They frequently prefer to stay where they were born, or where they have relatives, rather than take a better-paid job elsewhere.

In recent years, a campaign has been afoot – on both sides of the Atlantic – to get the public to accept unemployment itself as 'respectable'. Unemployment, we have been told, should not be regarded as the evil of our age but rather as a country's reward for increased efficiency. In other words, it is actually a virtue. In Britain, several ingenious schemes have been put forward, including one which proposes that the unemployed should be paid a proper living wage – a wage for not working. Carried to its logical conclusion, this means that before long 'full-time unemployed' would come to be regarded as a proper job. You could enter it in your passport and regard yourself as a highly esteemed member of the community – a man who helps his fellow-citizens by keeping out of their way.

I fancy, though, that some spoilsport would sooner or later start to worry about the harmful effects which paid-for idleness might have on your soul and try to find you things to do. I'm afraid there are an awfully large number of precedents. The ancient Egyptians diverted the hordes of unoccupied *fellahin* on to building the pyramids, and Hitler built the German *autobahns* on this same Cheops/Keynesian principle. More recently, a bird-watcher from Atlanta, Georgia, stood as a write-in presidential candidate for the 'Front Porch Party'. He ran on a ticket which proposed to put the unemployed to work boring holes in dead trees so that our feathered friends would have more convenient places to nest in.

Fortunately, there is no shortage of less strenuous pastimes. There are already quite a number of people who are unemployed in the traditional sense of the word, but not jobless. Actors, novelists, poachers, playboys, and criminals all come into this category. They would, I imagine, be first in the queues of those asking for a 'living wage'. As far as I can see, there would be nothing to stop you joining them. Another well-tried method would be to form a committee or association. There are already a vast number of bodies which serve no purpose other than to keep their officers busy.

Not least, you could form a non-trading company. I know several companies which ceased trading several decades ago, but still maintain boards of directors. They meet once a month, chat about the weather, collect their fees, and go home again. Making unemployment 'respectable' clearly requires only a little imagination. Indeed, thinking up suitable schemes might itself be a way of keeping you busy.

There are, of course, people who think the whole campaign is a lot of nonsense. They insist that unemployment is contemptible, and want governments to do everything in their power to keep us all producing cars, engines, ships, and sprockets. How old-fashioned can you get?

## REGULATOR

The power given to a Chancellor to impose or remove an extra tax or surcharge on existing taxes. Developed in the early sixties, it is an attempt to get away from the absurd idea that a Chancellor can get up, on a day in April, and announce a set of regulations which will do for the rest of the financial year. Modern economic management calls for much more frequent adjustments, and the regulator is a way of varying certain tax rates at any given time, without going through the elaborate motions of seeking parliamentary approval. One result is that we nowadays tend to have one or more 'mini-Budgets'. Newspapers usually jump to the conclusion that things have gone wrong; in fact, they are merely part of an effort to avoid sudden sharp changes of direction. It was dubbed 'a touch on the tiller' when Reginald Maudling was Chancellor of the Exchequer, and has many enthusiastic supporters. Some economists, however, argue that once-a-year changes have an important psychological impact which should not be lost: people tend to respond more readily to decisive leads than to constant adjustments.

## RIGGING THE MARKET

An attempt to create an artificial situation in the market for a particular share. This can be done in a number of ways, but an essential prerequisite is a 'thin' market, meaning that there are not many shares in circulation. It's clearly difficult to rig the market in a popular share like ICI or Marks and Spencer, because a significant increase in price could bring out sellers.

But a small family-controlled company, which has marketed only a small proportion of its shares, is in a very different position. The outside speculator may very well succeed in pushing up the price by buying a number of shares, and spreading rumours of an impending 'favourable development'. This is share-pushing, pure and simple. Under Stock Exchange rules, the people who deal in shares are compelled to deliver stock once they have entered into a firm verbal commitment. The stock may not actually be in their possession, and they usually rely on the probability that a higher price will bring in sellers. (This is what financial journalists mean when they say that the market is 'short of stock'.) The rigger can afford to play a waiting game. If he has picked the right victim, the response, in terms of price, will be quite out of proportion to the amount of

F

buying. He waits until the price has risen to a totally artificial level and then sells all or part of his holding. The chief losers, as a rule, are less skilful speculators who thought they were on to a good thing but have simply been taken along for the ride. (See also: TIPSTER.)

## RIGHTS ISSUE
An issue of new shares to existing shareholders, who have the 'right' to buy them at a certain price. There may, or may not, be an element of profit in such an issue; in any event, shareholders need not necessarily take the new shares up. It is, however, well to consult one's stockbroker because inaction may mean a loss. Rights issues are a useful way for companies to raise money, especially at times when the market is bouyant. But they are not always popular with investors, and the share price often falls slightly when one is announced.

## SATISFACTORY
The most overworked word in a company chairman's vocabulary. It can be used to cover a multitude of possibilities. At one extreme it may mean a 30% rise in profits; the Chairman only calls it 'satisfactory progress' because he doesn't want any shareholders to think that success is making him complacent. At the other, it may mean a 10% fall in profits. The Chairman will simply blame the Government, or the weather, or whatever else happens to be handy and announce that the figures are 'satisfactory in the circumstances'. Used in forecasts, the word is almost meaningless and ought to be banned. Investors should certainly not allow themselves to be misled by it.

## SCARCE CURRENCY CLAUSE
A clause in the articles of the International Monetary Fund which enables member countries to impose discriminatory import restrictions against a country whose currency has been officially declared 'scarce'. The idea was to have some weapon against governments which deliberately kept their currencies undervalued, so that their exporters would have an extra advantage in world trading markets

The offended parties would complain to the International Monetary Fund, which would then give its official blessing to retaliatory steps. It was thought, of course, that the mere threat would normally be enough to achieve the desired effect. The clause, certainly, has been invoked on very few occasions. When President Nixon took action, in the summer of 1971, to 'protect the dollar', he did not single out the Japanese – even though the yen could very easily have been declared a 'scarce currency'. He imposed a general import surcharge on foreign products instead. This, no doubt, was partly because Washington has disliked the clause ever since the postwar years when the obvious candidate for discrimination was the dollar.

## SCARSDALE FATS
Nickname said to have been invented by Boston institutions for a heavyweight Wall Street stockbroker who specializes in brain-picking sessions over lunch. I am not one to give away true identities, but I was once approached by a heavyweight Wall Street stockbroker called Bob Brimberg and asked to attend just such a lunch. He suggested that I should talk to his guests, about the pound or whatever else took my fancy, and added that for this rather pleasant duty (I was then a financial editor, in New York to gather views for my column) I would be paid a fee of $500. In London one is expected to talk for free, so I accepted with alacrity. Half-way through lunch, Mr Brimberg's *modus operandi* became brilliantly clear. He made a point of inviting investment managers whose business he hoped to get to come and listen, over the scampi and iced water, to a guest who would reveal all. I hardly matched up to his usual standard – my immediate predecessor had been Everett Dirksen – but I gather that my fee matched my status. Mr Brimberg was solely interested in making contact with people who wouldn't have bothered with him otherwise, and we were the bait. I admired the way he went to work, but I'm bound to say that when, a few months later, he tried the same in London it was not a success. At his request, and for a substantial fee, I invited twenty leading City investment managers to the Savoy for dinner. They had a good time – until Mr Brimberg made it clear that they were expected to get down to business. English City gentlemen are as eager as anyone

else to make money (and often more ruthless than their American rivals) but they like to keep up the pretence that it's a sideline – not to be discussed, in blunt fashion, over brandy and cigars.

## SCRIP ISSUE

An issue of new shares to shareholders without their having to put up any further money. More popularly known as share 'bonus', a somewhat misleading term because it gives the impression that people are getting something extra. The American equivalent, stock split, is more aptly named because this is exactly what happens – the stock is split. A one-for-one share 'bonus' means, for example, that you end up with twice as many shares, but with each share worth only half as much as before. The market automatically adjusts the price to allow for the issue. The same happens with dividends. Scrip issues, or stock splits, are nevertheless popular because they do tend to have a beneficial effect. New investors, for example, are often put off by a 'heavy' price – say £3 or £4 a share – and buy much more readily if it is split. This, of course, helps the existing holders. Company boards, moreover, often try to give investors at least a modest effective increase in dividend.

A good way of judging whether a company has scope for a share bonus is to add up the total of its reserves and compare it with the par value of the ordinary shares. If the reserves are substantially larger, the board may wish to bring them 'into line' with the equity.

## SECOND MORTGAGE

A way of raising credit, with your house as security. If you are buying your home through a building society, and have only a few years to go, you may well be tempted to take out a second mortgage, either to buy a car or boat, or to pay for some other fancy. This is usually done through a mortgage broker but a number of finance houses – such as United Dominions Trust – are now advertising their services directly to the public. It's a controversial business, partly because some mortgage brokers have, in the past, forced more credit on borrowers than they really wanted, and partly because interest rates tend to be considerably higher than on first mortgages. People in the business claim that second mortgages

'have become respectable', but even so it pays to take care. Try
your bank manager first: he may be more helpful than you think.

## SECURITIES AND EXCHANGE COMMISSION
An official watchdog, popularly known as the SEC, which is supposed
to regulate the securities industry in the United States. It has considerable powers, and occasionally uses them. Over the years,
however, the SEC has pushed Wall Street towards a policy of 'self-
regulation' – a bureaucratic euphemism, some say, for no regulation
whatever. Much the same is true of Britain, which has no official
body like the SEC. The Stock Exchange Council, the Bank of England and other city bodies usually try to ensure that the rules are
followed: in obvious cases of abuse, the Board of Trade is em-
powered to step in. There is also a City Fraud Squad, made up of
policemen with accountancy degrees or other financial qualifications, which watches out for currency frauds and other infringe-
ments of the law.

## SELL HALF
Advice given by professional investment advisers who want to keep
their clients happy. I once knew a city editor who made this his
stock answer to every inquiry. He was highly popular. Every stockbroker and financial journalist knows that advice to sell *everything*
is risky. If the shares go up afterwards, you will be bitterly criticized
for depriving your customer of an easy profit. If you make your
advice public – either through a financial column or through a
monthly stockbrokers' circular – people will accuse you of deliberately driving the price down. 'Sell half' is the kind of compromise
solution that appeals to every Englishman.

Professionals know, of course, that selling at the right moment is
an essential part of successful investment – and even more of
speculation. Amateurs tend to care too much about the price they
paid; if they show a loss, they usually hang on in the desperate hope
that, sooner or later, the shares will get back to the old level. Sometimes they never do. More often, it takes years to reach the original
price. By cutting his loss, and re-investing in a more promising
share, the holder could have done much better.

The way to speculate successfully is to take a long series of small losses and one great big profit. Sell if you bought a share for a particular reason, and that reason proves to be wrong. Don't invent other reasons for holding on.

## SELLERS' MARKET

One in which conditions are favourable to sellers, usually because demand is bigger than supply. If people want more copies of this book than the publisher has printed, and he is unwilling to produce more, he is in a sellers' market. He may raise the price, and generally do his best to exploit the situation. Sellers' markets are caused by many factors. In wartime, rationing and transport difficulties may be the chief reasons. If rapid inflation – too much money chasing too few goods – is added to this, sellers tend to have it all their own way. In peacetime, the manufacturer of a novel and attractive new product may deliberately restrict deliveries to retailers, so that he can keep the price high. It's usually not very long before a rival provides some competition, but sometimes a sellers' market may continue for years.

A buyers' market is exactly the opposite: it may arise from overproduction, or a sudden fall in demand, and is usually associated with business recessions.

## SERVICE CONTRACT

An arrangement devised to ensure that key executives stay in their jobs. It may cover anything from one to five years. Good men are not easy to come by, and sensible firms try to make sure that they are not lured away by rivals. Sometimes, of course, things go wrong. An executive may not live up to his early promise, or he may disagree with the rest of the board on how the company should be run. The service contract can, in those circumstances, be terminated on payment of compensation.

Takeover bids and mergers have added an interesting new twist to the game. Directors who have reason to suspect that someone may try to bid for their firm invariably take a quick look at their service contracts. If they have only short periods to run, they vote themselves new five-year agreements. In other words, the bidder may find that, if he succeeds in winning control, it will cost him a very large sum of money to change the board. There are several examples of bids which were withdrawn after the board's stratagem became known; the people who suffered were, of course, the unsuspecting shareholders.

## SHARE OPTIONS

A means of giving senior employees a share in the prosperity of a company. The basic idea is simple: it's easier to attract the right managerial talent, and to keep it keen, if one can offer more than the usual salary and perks. So you give your key people an option to take up shares, requiring from them only a nominal sum for the privilege. If they rise in value, they are free to sell and make a profit.

The Labour Party has always treated this kind of thing with much suspicion, regarding it as merely another big business fiddle. In 1966, during Labour's term of office, the law was changed so that all gains from options given by a company to its employees and directors were charged to income tax. It meant, in effect, that options lost their value overnight. But then, to take their place, a whole range of share incentive schemes came into effect. Some of them were highly ingenious; in any event, the 1966 Act was defeated. In 1972, Tory Chancellor Tony Barber decided that the Labour Act had been 'altogether too drastic' and announced that, in future, gains would be subject to capital gains tax and not income tax. The Chancellor stipulated, however, that all option schemes would have to be approved by the Inland Revenue and laid down a series of conditions which commentators attacked as 'onerous'.

Necessary incentive or big business fiddle? The truth, as economists like to say, probably lies somewhere in between. It is a 'fiddle' of sorts. On the other hand there's much to be said for giving the new breed of managers a better chance to build up the kind of capital needed to ensure financial independence. The need to play safe can, and does, stifle enterprise and gives too much power to the institutions who control the purse strings.

## SHELL

Stock market term for a company which has very little left in the
way of assets, but whose shares are still quoted on the Stock Exchange. It is, literally, a 'shell'. As such, it may appeal to businessmen who are interested in getting a market quote through the back
door. The basic strategy is simple: buy control, inject earnings and
assets into it, change the name, and presto! the company rises like a
phoenix from the ashes and its shares go ahead.

In Britain, rubber and tea plantation companies have for many
years been the classic prey of 'shell' operations. Mostly their shares
are quoted at a few pence each but have a wide marketability so that
sizeable shareholdings can be accumulated before the buying is
detected, either by shrewd market men or the Board itself. The aim
is to get something like 30% or 40%, whether through steady buying in the market or through a deal to take over a family or boardroom holding. You then make an offer for the rest, sell some of the
unwanted assets (if there are any) and inject your own little operation – which may be engineering or some other activity far removed
from the world of tea and rubber. If you are known as an enter-
prising character, people will soon want to back you and, before
long, you will make a bid for some other company. In short, the
'shell' is gradually filled out with all sorts of profitable assets. Many
well-known companies started out this way. The Stock Exchange,
however, takes a much tougher line with 'shell' operations than it
used to and some of the former attraction has gone. Dealings in
shares is usually suspended until the company has fully proved its
new status; this can often last a considerable period of time.

## SHOE RIOT

One of the more extravagant phrases used by American retail firms
(in this case shoe shops) to attract customers. 'Storm' is another
favourite. A 'clothing storm' is considered to be a much more exciting concept than a mere sale. One advertisement which caught my
eye, not along ago, was aimed at the Greenwich Village set. 'We've
got a surplus hang-up', it announced, 'it comes on every time you
make the scene at Kaufman – where the in-look blows your mind
and keeps your bread cool.' They ought to try *that* at Harrods.

# SLUMP
The most dramatic of three stages in economic downturns – recession, depression, slump. Its outward symptoms are high unemployment, and a fall in production, profits and prices. Newspapers love the word, because it fits easily into a headline and tends to make a big impact. It therefore tends to be used more often than circumstances really justify. Slumps often follow a boom which has got out of hand; the first real sign of downturn sends people into a panic because they are over committed, and their reaction tends to have a chain effect. Governments nowadays try to avoid rapid changes from boom to slump by frequent adjustments in key factors such as interest rates and taxation, but experience shows that, once people have convinced themselves that things are bad, it takes a long time to restore confidence. (See BUSINESS CONFIDENCE and RECESSION.)

# SPECIAL DRAWING RIGHTS
In banking and academic circles, it's smart to call them 'SDR's'. In the newspaper world, they are usually known as 'paper gold'. Actually, they are neither gold nor paper but, very simply, an allocation of automatic credit lines which can be used between different countries. They serve as extra reserves at a time of balance of payments difficulties. They are not meant to be a *substitute* for getting the balance of payments right, nor are they a panacea for the problems of the international monetary system. SDR's are valuable chiefly because they represent a firm departure from man's slavery to gold, for so long the pivot of the system. The SDR scheme is administered by the International Monetary Fund (see page 108) and it took years to get agreement among the hundred-plus countries which belong to this twentieth-century version of a mutual aid society. Monetary puritans still dislike it.

# SPECULATOR
Every politician's favourite scapegoat. In the communist world he has long been officially designated villain. He loyally served Marx, Lenin and Mao Tse-tung – indeed, it is no exaggeration that, without him, the communist system might never have come into being. He was, and still is, the man everyone loves to hate.

The Soviets have never thanked the speculator, or at least acknowledged their debt to him. Nor, for that matter, have the Chinese. If there is one thing which unites this vast, mysterious country, it is a Peking-inspired-and-approved contempt for speculation. Next to the warlords of the Pentagon, the speculator is the one figure still clearly identifiable as the arch-enemy.

What really hurts, however, is that the speculator has, over the years, found himself increasingly condemned by his own side. The London Stock Exchange disowned him a long time ago. Needled by phrases like 'gambling casino' and 'speculators' paradise', the gentlemen who run this august institution insisted that they had never really approved of him. The Stock Exchange, we were told, existed to serve *investors* – worthy citizens prepared to back Britain by putting their life savings into solid blue chips. It did not, repeat not, exist to make money for idle, unscrupulous rascals who had no interest beyond buying and selling. I have never quite understood why the Stock Exchange should be so anxious to reject the profit motive. Backing Britain is all very well, but making a few thousand overnight is even better. Any member of the Stock Exchange who says otherwise is a hypocrite – or an idealist who should seek a different profession.

It was easier to accept the Macmillan Government's decision to punish speculators by introducing a new tax on capital gains. The Chancellor of the day was trying to get the unions' co-operation on wages and, like all those who followed him, he thought it could be won attacking their traditional enemy. It didn't work. The tax, however, stayed. So did ministerial dislike of the speculator. Harold Wilson used to get terribly angry about the 'manœuvring of odious speculators'; the successive 'waves of speculation'; the 'speculation at home and abroad'. In speech after speech he conjured up visions of a sinister, tightly-knit group of politically motivated men hell-bent on 'selling Britain short'. The speculator, it appeared, spent his day swigging brandy and communicating absurd gossip to Paris and Zürich. His sole interest was in bringing Labour – and, therefore, the country – to its ruin. When sterling was devalued in 1967, Harold naturally blamed the speculators. And guess who lost him the 1970 General Election? Right first time.

In 1971, President Nixon joined the game. Richard Nixon! Hero of the Republican party, titular head of the capitalist world. Generations of Americans have been brought up to believe in the virtues of making a fast buck. Every library has dozens of books on the subject. America might have much to apologize for – but speculation? Surely not. Yet here was Mr Nixon, condemning the poor speculator for 'waging all-out war against the dollar' and 'thriving on crises'.

Who are the speculators? In the currency field, mostly bankers paid to make the best use of their clients' money, or by the finance directors of big corporations who have entered into extensive commitments abroad. They don't like the word 'speculation'; in their book, it is called 'money management'. Businessmen, they say, do not have a patriotic duty to risk losses or forgo a possible profit: it's the job of governments to maintain confidence in currency. (See also BEAR.)

## SPIT

An organization existing solely in the mind of the author, but essential if we want to avoid chaos. SPIT is short for Society to Prevent the Initials Trend, and is dedicated to preserving Shakespeare's language from the relentless attacks of economists, businessmen, and bureaucrats. The human race, it seems, has an insatiable urge to set up more and more committees and organizations. And each one insists, sooner or later, on being known by its initials. We have UNO, UNESCO, NATO, SEATO, WHO, GATT, and NIBMAR, and we have innumerable trade organizations which feel deeply insulted if you don't immediately appreciate the significance of letters like BEMA and SIMA. The same applies if you visit the United States or Germany. The merger mania in industry ought to have cut down the number of initials, but the opposite is true. Faced with the need to find a new title which describes their extended range of activities, company boards invariably fall back on initials. Occasionally, some brave fellow makes a plea for originality, but is usually slapped down on the grounds that it would be tragic to lose the goodwill attached to a name built up over the years. Initials tend to be regarded as the next best thing. Ultimately, we may have to start talking in this crazy language, for fear of not being with it. 'Good morning, EBD. RST here. Have you seen that letter from UDT? They want to know if we have talked to BSA and WGI. They think IBI may be worth contacting too.' SOS!

## SQUARE MILE
London's financial district, better known as 'the City'. It was the original London, with a Royal Charter from William the Conqueror, and although few people now live there, it still keeps up the trappings of a separate existence. The City has its own Mayor, its own courts and police force, a long list of trade guilds, and an extraordinary range of ceremonials. Hard-headed money men see nothing ludicrous (or so it seems) in dressing up in medieval robes and chains, symbolizing offices which have long ceased to have any real meaning.

The ritual gives an impression of unity that is hardly justified by the facts. The Lord Mayor does not speak for the City, any more than the chairman of the Stock Exchange. The nearest thing to an official spokesman is the Governor of the Bank of England – but, given his close association with the government of the day, he is not generally accepted as the City's voice either. The plain fact is that the City has many different voices, and many different shades of opinion. A man from Lloyd's may never meet a stockbroker, even though they both work in the 'Square Mile'. A shipbroker may spend a lifetime in the City without once getting into a conversation with a commodity dealer. Yet both are part of the City – along with merchant bankers, fishmongers, accountants, experts in furs and diamonds, and insurance men. In recent years, too, a large number of foreigners have set up shop. There are well over a hundred foreign banks in the City, including the Moscow Narodny Bank. The Americans and Japanese have been particularly active: City wags now call one street 'Yankee Alley' and 'the Avenue of the Americas'. No one would dream of suggesting that they are part of some old boys' network. If there is a common factor, it is a belief in the power of money, and in the desirability of getting one's hands on a little more of it.

## STERLING AREA

Hangover from the days of Empire. When Britain went off the gold standard in 1931 (i.e. her paper money ceased to be interchangeable with gold) a number of countries which had strong financial ties with us decided to link the exchange value of their currencies to sterling rather than to the dollar. They included all the Commonwealth countries except Canada, the Scandinavian states, and various others such as Egypt and Portugal. When war broke out this 'sterling bloc', as it was known, was formally associated with us in a financial 'club' called the Sterling Area. Members agreed to conduct their trade with each other in sterling, and to ensure that trade and payments between them were relatively unrestricted. They also agreed to turn the bulk of their foreign exchange earnings into pounds, which they left in London; these 'sterling balances' formed the bulk of the reserves backing for their own currencies.

At one time, the Sterling Area was the financial cornerstone of the Empire and, more recently, it has helped to give the word 'Commonwealth' some meaning. But the arrangement has proved to be of less and less value. When sterling ran into trouble under the 1964–70 Labour Government, its role as a world currency made things worse. And our fellow club members became increasingly nervous. They were expected to help – but, as I was reminded by Mr William McMahon, then in charge of Australia's finances, 'a friend in need is a bloody nuisance'. In recent years club members have increasingly gone their own way, and in 1972 the Tory Government announced that 'for the time being' exchange controls (i.e. restrictions on transfers of money in and out of Britain) would be extended to the Sterling Area. The only exceptions were Eire, the Channel Isles, and the isle of Man – some empire! The Bank of England insisted that the measures were 'temporary', but with Britain committed to Common Market membership the general verdict was that 'the Sterling Area is dead'.

## SURVIVAL

The art, usually complex, of remaining a Higher Executive. Memorize the following seven basic rules, and you'll be all right:

### (1) Don't become a big businessman

This is an elementary precaution, but it's remarkable how many intelligent people ignore it. Experience shows that life is much safer just below the top. In Whitehall the permanent secretaries wield more power, earn more money, and stay around longer than their alleged, over-publicized political masters. In industry the men who have charge of the purse – usually accountants – have developed an enviable resistance to purges. Choose your place, well away from the founder's portrait, and refuse to budge. Resist all offers of promotion – and arrange to be out of town whenever important decisions are being taken.

### (2) Cultivate the City

Because that's where the power lies. The City institutions are the biggest shareholders in industry, and they have become significantly more militant. When a company runs into trouble, it's the City which forces changes in management.

### (3) Don't talk, listen

It's easy to talk yourself into trouble. You may, for example, object to some proposal on the grounds that it is both absurd and illogical. This, as any skilled survivor will tell you, is naïve. Your fellow executives will never forgive you. Sooner or later you will be tempted to present your own proposal. It will be accepted with alacrity – and, three months later, you will be held to account for the consequences. Be non-committal. Listen. People love good listeners: they tend to be praised as great conversationalists.

### (4) Don't say no

Superiors are often heard to say that they don't want yes-men. This is a lie: they do. If the top man wants to win an argument, let him. But it's good strategy, just occasionally, to make him wait a few seconds for your 'yes'. Darryl Zanuck once snapped at an over-eager assistant: 'Don't say yes until I've finished talking.'

## (5) Beware of politicians

Ministers move around so fast that it doesn't pay to get friendly. If you are known to be on good terms with one, the next one will almost certainly want to make an example out of you – just to show that he disagrees with his predecessor. If a minister enters a room, try to make an excuse and leave. Refuse to be drawn into making an open statement of support for any party: if, by some mischance, you are forced to make a speech stick to platitudes used and accepted by both sides.

## (6) Never resign

'Only fools resign', Lord Beaverbrook once told me – and, of course, he was right. Most people offer their resignation in the certainty that it won't be accepted. They consider themselves indispensable, and are surprised to find that others don't agree. By then it's usually too late. Don't let anyone goad you into resigning: remember that people who leave voluntarily rarely collect compensation. If you want to leave, goad them into sacking you. If you want to stay, ignore their hints. It's surprising how many executives threatened with dismissal have kept their jobs by pretending to be deaf.

## (7) Ignore failures

They may be nice fellows – indeed, they almost invariably are – but it's unwise to associate with losers. You've heard of guilt by association? Well then.

## STAG

Next to bulls and bears, the most ferocious of the Stock Exchange's animals. Well, he's not all that ferocious, really. It would be fascinating to know why the early, brandy-swigging stockbrokers were so desperately anxious to pick these virility symbols: why not pigs, ducks, and geese?

A stag is one who subscribes for new issues on the market, not with the noble aim of holding them as an investment, but with the base desire to name a quick killing (Aha! There's your answer). He looks out for companies whose shares are coming onto the market for the first time, and if they seem likely to appeal to investors he fills in an application form. Or, more probably, several application forms. They are published in one or more newspapers (*The Financial Times* is always certain to carry one) and hardened stags have been known to fill in up to a hundred forms using all types of names. Some are always genuine: it's marvellous how many aunts you can find when money is involved. Others are pure invention. The Stock Exchange, alas, has clamped down on this kind of activity and the stag's life is nowadays much more difficult. The world, sad to say, is full of spoilsports.

## STAGFLATION

A hybrid meaning that the economy is making no headway – stagnating – and having inflation at the same time. It's really the worst of both worlds and difficult to cure.

## STATISTICS

Tabulated numerical facts. We trust them more than we trust politicians. People lie, but figures tell the truth. Or so it's said. The reality is different. Statistics can be made to dance to any tune you want to play. You can put favourable factors in, and leave others out. You can adjust, revise, ignore. And you can twist the end product. Successive election campaigns have shown how eminently twistable statistics can be. No one is lying; he is interpreting figures in a way favourable to his own argument. To one party, an £800 million balance of payments deficit is the most frightful catastrophe. To another, it is a minor problem.

In 1969, the Polish Embassy in London – of all people – discovered that Britain's Board of Trade, with its computers and highly trained officials, had somehow managed to mislay £11 million a month for the past six years. It meant that, throughout the long and costly financial crisis, we had consistently underrated our strength. Indeed, one Treasury official was quoted as saying that devaluation would have been unnecessary if the error had been discovered sooner. The people who compile statistics know, of course, how unreliable they can be. This is why Whitehall always makes a point of drawing attention to the small print. Civil servants have little time for ministers and impatient industrialists who want 'one figure, with no ifs and buts'. At best, figures are no more than a guide. At worst, they point away from the truth.

Statistics, alas, have increasingly become a substitute for argument, and a good memory for facts and figures is generally regarded as superior to thought. People have come to accept this to such an extent, that you can get away with making up figures on the spot, as long as you sound confident enough in your delivery. Try it next time you get into a boring argument at a dinner party. Do me one favour, though. When you have won your case, confess what you have been doing. Your fellow men won't thank you for exposing their gullibility, but you will have done them a service.

## STOP-GO
A familiar feature of the British post-war financial and economic scene. It means, very simply, sharp changes in direction at uncomfortably frequent intervals. The pattern goes something like this. The economy is sluggish, unemployment is high, and the Government is urged to do something about it. It cuts taxes, makes credit easier, lowers interest rates, and generally sets the lights to 'go'. A few months later, though, it appears that this bold strategy is damaging the balance of payments. We import too much, pay ourselves too much in wages, and generally live beyond our long-term means. The pound comes under pressure, and we are right in the middle of another financial crisis. To counter it, the Government raises taxes, makes credit harder to get, boosts interest rates, and generally sets the lights to 'stop'.

Stop-go has happened so often that businessmen have become highly sceptical about government forecasts. We need a period of sustained advance, say five years, before most of them will really believe that we have managed to get away from it.

## STUDY IN DEPTH
Anything that takes time. Governments like to use it to postpone decisions which may, for the moment, be too costly or politically awkward. By ordering a 'study in depth', and announcing the fact to the public, they can convey the impression that something is being done. Ministers usually know perfectly well that the study will

achieve nothing, and that it will join earlier studies on some White-hall shelf, unloved and forgotten. But that's not the point: if it keeps critics quiet, it has achieved its purpose. A recurring example is a 'study in depth' of the endemic unemployment problem of Britain's regions. The Government has commissioned endless studies on the subject, and is fully aware that nothing short of growth in the economy as a whole will ever provide a satisfactory answer. And yet, each time unemployment rises to embarrassing levels, it reacts by ordering yet another 'study in depth'. We are asked not to be cynical about our politicians, and perhaps it's unfair that we should be. They are, after all, to a very considerable extent at the mercy of events. But it becomes increasingly difficult to go along with this particular charade.

## SUBSIDIARY
Also known as 'offshoot'. A company in which another holds more than half of the voting shares. This gives it the right to appoint directors and direct boardroom decisions. Many subsidiaries are 'wholly owned'; Ford of Britain, for example, is a wholly owned subsidiary of Ford US. But there are also companies in which the public has minority stake. The minority shareholder has certain rights, but he is to a large extent at the mercy of the 'parent company' or 'holding company' which exercises control. Dividends, for ex-ample, may be deliberately kept down. On the other hand, he some-times benefits from a major expansion programme made possible by the parent's vast resources, or from the injection of technological expertise. It is always possible, too, that the parent will one day decide to make an offer for the minority holdings – in which case there could be a useful capital gain.

## SUBSIDY
Government grants of money to a company, local authority, or industry. Most governments nowadays make considerable use of subsidies. They may, for example, decide that the public interest demands low prices for farm products, and pay farmers the dif-ference between a mutually agreed level and what they are able to

get in the open market. Or they may use state money to finance public housing projects, and to charge low-income tenants a rent which any normal landlord would regard as uneconomic. Aid to regions, to make up for lack of raw materials or some other weakness, has also grown more common. And, of course, governments frequently subsidize public services such as transport, and special projects which are thought worthwhile from a national point of view – such as space travel – but which are not viable on strictly commercial considerations. Theatres, art galleries, museums and many other useful features of modern civilized life all benefit from government subsidies.

In theory, there is no limit to the game. There is certainly no shortage of worthy causes, and of demands for help. In practice, though, governments have to draw the line somewhere if they want to stay in power. Subsidies are part of government expenditure, and high expenditure can only be sustained, in the long run, by high taxation.

## TAKEOVER BID
An attempt by one company to buy control of another. Because the phrase implies aggression, most bidders prefer to use the more conciliatory word 'merger'. The end result, though, tends to be much the same.

Bids and mergers fall into three main categories, depending largely on the company making the offer. First, and historically most logical, there is the offer made by a company for another doing the same kind of work. This is known as a horizontal merger. If, for example, two companies manufacturing lawn mowers decided to get together, it would be a horizontal merger. It may arise from several motives. The bidder may want to reduce competition and increase his share of the market. He may want to acquire added plant and equipment similar to his own, in order to take advantage of growing demand for his products. Or he may simply want to achieve the economies to be had from pooling resources. Costs per unit tend to decline as the scale of production increases, and mergers can be a quick way of securing cost reductions.

The second type of merger is known as vertical. It covers the linking of firms at immediately related stages of production and distribution. The buyer may merge with or acquire a company on which he either relies for his supplies, or to which he sells much of his output. The one deal will ensure that raw materials and components essential to his basic business will always be available, at a price over which he has control. The other will put him closer to the consumer. It may, for example, enable him to cut out the wholesaler and deal directly with the retail trade.

The third type of merger is the conglomerate, and this involves the merger or acquisition of a company whose activities are in an entirely different sphere (see page 51).

Takeover bids and mergers are as old as business itself. There have been several 'merger waves', on both sides of the Atlantic, during the past one hundred years. Many of industry's big names are composite creations. But, as I showed in my book *Merger Mania*, the outcome is often disappointing. The 'economies of scale' tend to take longer to achieve than the bidder would have investors believe at the time of the deal – and size can produce all kinds of problems. The largest company is not necessarily the most efficient or even the most profitable. If size is the prime objective the company can topple under its own weight.

Many companies, too, merge for reasons which have little or nothing to do with industrial logic. Big companies often buy up others solely to prevent a rival from getting them first. This may produce a merger which is structurally all wrong. The same goes for purely defensive marriages, arranged to avoid the embraces of an unwanted partner. It's astonishing how many deals are based on hunches rather than careful calculation; the age of allegedly sophisticated management still has a large number of top executives flying by the seat of their pants.

## TAX AVOIDANCE
The lawful part of what is more popularly known as 'tax dodging'. The law makes a clear distinction between evasion and avoidance. Evasion is deliberate fraud – you know you ought to declare, say, a capital gain on a stock market operation, but do not do so. Avoidance is to know the nature of the tax, and ways of skating around it

through full use of allowances and one or another of the many complex financial schemes – all strictly legal – thought up by clever tax accountants. A famous edict by a Scottish judge, Lord Clyde, holds that 'no man in this country is under the smallest obligation, moral or other, so to arrange his legal relations to his business or his property as to enable the Inland Revenue to put the largest shovel into his stores'.

Even so, an awful lot of nonsense is talked about allegedly despicable behaviour of people who choose to arrange their affairs in such a way as to suit themselves rather than the Inland Revenue. Film stars who choose to make their home Switzerland, rather than the country of their birth, are frequently accused of being unpatriotic. And there is, invariably, much criticism of wealthy people who find perfectly legitimate ways of minimizing estate duty.

In France, during 1972, a 'tax scandal' blew up around the Prime Minister, M. Chaban-Delmas. The Paris satirical weekly, *Le Canard Enchaîné,* alleged that he had managed to escape all taxation from 1966 to 1970. The Finance Minister, M. Giscard D'Estaing, went on national television to explain how this sort of thing was possible under the French system of tax credits, and pointed out that it was open to everyone else to do the same. In other words, if the affair struck people as unjust, it was the system which deserved the blame, not the individual. There is, arguably, something wrong with a tax structure which allows highly placed – and wealthy – people to get away with not paying any taxes. Perhaps the affair will lead to changes. M. Chaban-Delmas was, however, well within his lawful rights, and not even his fiercest critics dared to claim that the Government had rigged the system with an eye to purely personal gain. No one owes a duty to pay more than the law demands; it's only evasion of the law which can cause you trouble.

## TAX HAVEN
Any place which helps foreigners to avoid paying taxes, or at least to keep a substantially bigger part of their income than they would be allowed to do at home. Switzerland is perhaps the best-known example; its unique combination of political stability, banking secrecy, highly developed financial expertise, and low rate of tax

have attracted many famous residents. Foreigners living in Switzerland but not gainfully employed there are taxed solely on an amount equivalent to five times the rental value of their property. The tiny principality of Liechtenstein is another well-known tax haven, but it does not encourage new residents: its main appeal is to corporations. One popular corporate device is the foreign-based 'holding company'. A foreign firm may transfer money earned outside its own country to, say, a holding company in Liechtenstein. Such a company has to have a local director, but there is no reason why it should not be wholly owned by the foreign firm. The money thus transferred by the owner will usually avoid most, if not all taxation. The Bahamas also offers a wide range of services and are more pleasant to live in than other tax havens. There is no income tax, no capital gains tax, and no estate duty. But if you haven't yet made your first million, there is one drawback: the high cost of living. This, indeed, tends to be a problem with most tax havens (it certainly applies to Switzerland) and can be a nuisance. There's not much point, after all, in cutting your tax bill if all the other bills soar.

Nearer home, the Channel Islands and the Isle of Man both rate as tax havens because they have no capital gains tax or estate duty, and income tax is substantially less than in areas which are under the direct jurisdiction of the Inland Revenue and the Treasury. In the Channel Islands income tax has been pegged at 20p in the pound since 1940; in the Isle of Man, the rate is 21p.

## TAX LOSS SELLING

Losses made on an investment can be set off against capital gains tax. If you sell stocks or property on which you show a loss, so that you can establish a claim for relief on profits made elsewhere, the process is known as tax loss selling. Everyone makes investment mistakes but the tax loss takes some of the sting out of it by letting you profit a little bit more on other successful investments.

## TAX REFORMS

A device used by politicians to help with elections. Having so many taxes around has not only enabled governments to keep spending what they like, but has also made it easy for politicians to pose as our saviours. Governments get elected, every few years, because they promise to deliver us from taxes introduced by other governments. And Chancellors of the Exchequer win our gratitude by announcing 'far-reaching reforms of the whole tax system'.

Most of us accept without protest that taxes are a necessary evil. We think ourselves lucky if a Chancellor manages to 'give us a little more' – a phrase invented by politicians to disguise the fact that, in reality, he is simply allowing us to *keep* a little more of what we earn. But we do not dispute the Government's right to levy taxes, to dispose of the revenue in ways which may run counter to our individual wishes, and to make all kinds of moral judgments in doing so. Nor do we challenge its right to pry into our personal affairs, and to haul us up in court to answer whatever charge the Commissioners decide to make against us. We not only agree that the Government can do all this, but share its indignation that some people should try to skip through the net by moving to Switzerland or to the Bahamas. In short, successive governments have brainwashed us into accepting that the tax burden as a whole is not only inevitable, but also morally correct. It was not always so. Earlier generations put up a long and splendid struggle against taxation. If they had not done so, we might never have had a Parliament, and America might not have won its independence.

The history of taxation is full of cunning tricks played on a gullible electorate. A favourite dodge, for example, has been to use national emergencies as a pretext for introducing temporary taxes which, somehow, turned out to be permanent. This is how we first got income tax, in 1799. This is how we got purchase tax during the Second World War. The introduction of the Excise, during the much earlier Civil War, opened the way for an extraordinary range of devices, including a hearth tax and a window tax. The puritans invented it, but the Excise stayed on when the monarchy was restored in 1660 – and, of course, remains with us today. Among its many advantages, from the Government's point of view, is that few people realize just how much they hand over in this indirect way. Could you say, without looking up Custom and Excise Tables, how much duty you are paying on a bottle of Scotch? Or even on a packet of cigarettes?

## TECHNOLOGICAL GAP

First discovered by the Italians, who dubbed it *il gap tecnologico* and later advanced as one of the chief reasons why Britain should be in the Common Market. The 'gap' is between European and American techniques of management and technology. An OECD report in 1967 showed that the US spends six times as much on research and development as the Common Market and three times as much as Western Europe. Besides spending more, it was also getting better value for the money spent, which was devoted to well-defined ends, whereas the European countries tended to be spread too thinly over many unrelated areas and even lost altogether in abandoned projects like the TSR-2 in Britain and sundry joint enterprises which became too expensive. One result of the technological gap, the report noted, was a rapid increase in American control of the most advanced and fastest-growing branches of European industry. Soon after the report was published, the EEC's Council of Ministers agreed that the Six's scientific and technological research in certain fields should be coordinated, and Mr Wilson – then Prime Minister – made a speech in which he offered the Community a seven-point technology plan as a basis for joint action. The Wilson plan was never followed up, and European cooperation still leaves much to be desired. Indeed, the gap still seems to be widening.

## TIMES-SOTHEBY INDEX

An index which tries to measure the market value of works of art. Art, of course, is one of the more traditional forms of investment. The art galleries and museums maintain that they pay vast sums of money for paintings because they like art. There are also one or two eccentric private collectors who share their view. But this is the kind of sentimental, old-fashioned approach which the City rightly deplores.

There are many sound reasons for spending a king's ransom on a bit of old canvas, and art has nothing to do with any of them. It is merely the label which Art Investment Trusts put on their stock-in-trade. The main reason for buying an expensive painting is that it will go up in price. It is, or should be, a hedge against inflation. Possession of one or two fashionable paintings is also good for business. It not only confirms that the owner is wealthy, but also proves that he has shrewd judgment. A man who can pick paintings which appreciate in value is clearly the kind of chap one ought to back. The wealthy owner of a masterpiece, moreover, can insist that no one reproduces it, for chocolate boxes or cigarette cards, without mentioning his name. This can add up to thousands of pounds' worth of free publicity. Banks are enthusiastic buyers of paintings, because they help to project the right image. If a bank wants to stress that it is well-established and solid, it buys an old master. If it wants to demonstrate that it is swinging and with-it, it buys ultra-modern.

Modern paintings have been fashionable in recent years because banks are wooing young people. An additional factor is that you tend to get more for your money: modern artists are generous with canvas. The Chase Manhattan Bank, like others, has a special art committee which buys paintings for its rapidly expanding international network of branches. There's even an art committee at the International Monetary Fund. The lesson for painters is clear: be modern, stock up with large frames, and keep in mind, at all times, your painting's value as an investment.

## TIPSTER

Impolite, but accurate, word for someone who makes his living by telling others what to buy. A popular figure at cocktail parties and afternoon teas. Stock market tipsters tend to be the élite, because the Stock Exchange has a cachet which race tracks and betting shops can't match, but they are not necessarily more scientific. They listen to rumours, back hunches, study balance sheets (which are usually out of date by the time they're published) and cultivate contacts in industry and the City. Some are unscrupulous: they buy a certain share, plug it, and get out at a profit as soon as the price goes up. City Editors seldom do this (honest) because they know how easily they could be found out. I know of only one case where a city editor played the market in this way. Market professionals noticed that each time a certain share was tipped, the same broker appeared just beforehand with a buying order and reappeared again just afterwards to sell. Inquiries were made, the identity of his client was discovered, a complaint was lodged with the Stock Exchange

Council, the Council informed the man's Editor, and the Editor sacked him on the spot.

Successful share tipping is not as easy as people make out. There is a considerable element of hit-and-miss about it, and even experts frequently get caught. On Wall Street some professionals put their trust in astrology and I once met a banker who solemnly declared that the stock market closely followed the rise and fall in hemlines. In Britain computers are being used to weigh up the 'form' of shares, but you'd be amazed how many people still rely on a pin. There are, of course, various ways of giving one's tip a good start. The most obvious is to pick a share in which there is a 'thin' market. Newcomers offer a fairly wide range of choice. A small, promising firm may want a share quotation. It puts the minimum percentage asked for by the Stock Exchange on the market. Because it is a go-ahead concern, they are snapped up by investors and held on a long-term basis. This means that, at any given time, the supply of stock is limited. If the company produces excellent results, or a share tipster repeatedly draws attention to the high quality of the management, a number of other people may be tempted to have a go. Even a small amount of buying can, in these circumstances, produce quite a sharp rise.

Much the best way of establishing one's reputation as a tipster is to use what I call the 'grapeshot' method. You tip thirty shares at the start of the year, on the principle that there's safety in numbers. They can't *all* go wrong. For good measure, you continue to produce a steady stream of tips during the months that follow. At the end of the year, you simply mention the few which have done well. The other few hundred shares can be conveniently forgotten; no one wants to hear about failures.

Timing is essential to successful share tipping, as to so much else. I have, over the years, developed the basic rule: when everyone praises a share for weeks, and the price moves up sharply, I become extremely cautious. After a lengthy period of popularity, a great many people are waiting to cash in their profit. They continue to talk enthusiastically about the shares, in the hope that others will come in and drive the price higher still, but they are eager to be out at the right moment. The founder of the Rothschild family once said he had made his fortune by always selling too soon: an awful lot of speculators try to do the same. (See also SPECULATOR; LONG-TERM.)

## TRADE GAP

The gap between a country's imports and exports. It's often confused with the balance of payments, and many people wrongly assume it to be the equivalent of a nation's balance sheet. In fact, it is only one of the items – though, admittedly, often the most important one. Nations like the United States and Britain, for example, have always had a large income from investments abroad, and from service trades like banking, insurance, and shipping. Britain had a trade gap throughout the second half of the nineteenth century, generally regarded as the peak period of her prosperity. It only became a problem when, in later years, overseas investment declined and governments spent more abroad than the country could really afford. (See also BALANCE OF PAYMENTS, DEVALUATION and INVISIBLES.)

## TRANSITIONAL PERIOD

A period following Britain's entry into the Common Market, during which she tries to find out what she has let herself in for. Officially, a device for allowing each country to adjust itself gradually to new rules and regulations.

## TREASURY BILL

A piece of paper issued in denominations of £5,000, £10,000, and £50,000 which entitles its holder to payment, normally in ninety-one days' time, of the appropriate sum. Introduced in 1877, when the Chancellor of the day had some difficulty in raising finance on what he considered to be reasonable terms, it is the means by which the Government borrows for short periods. Bills are put up for sale each week and offers (the City prefers the word tenders) are invited for them. The weekly total may be several hundred million pounds depending on the Government's needs at any given time. The need may arise because its tax receipts fall short of Government spending or, more likely, because the timing of its receipts (which are heaviest in January and July) does not coincide with its pattern of constant spending. Demand usually comes from discount houses, merchant banks and other City institutions with short-term funds to spare. Large industrial and commercial firms also show increasing interest. The Treasury allocates the bills to the highest bidders. If necessary, the City's discount houses (see page 65) undertake to buy the lot. The Government, therefore, is always certain of being able to meet its financial needs.

## TREATY OF ROME

Strictly speaking, not one treaty but two. Signed by six countries (Belgium, France, Germany, Italy, Luxemburg and the Netherlands) in March 1957, they created two Communities: a European Economic Community (EEC) to bring into being a single market for all goods and develop a common economic policy, and a European Atomic Energy Community (Euratom) to further the use of nuclear energy in Europe for peaceful purposes. Headquarters were set up in Brussels.

The EEC soon became popularly known as the Common Market. It is an apt description, because of the many objectives laid down in the Treaty of Rome, the creation of a single market, unhampered by customs duties, has actually come about. Economic unity has been much harder to achieve. There is still no European company law, no common currency, no freedom from exchange control. With one or two exceptions, such as the agricultural system, economic and financial policies continue to be made at the national level. Political union seems even further away: there is a European parliament, but no one pays much attention to it. In short, the 'Europe' visualized by idealists when the Treaty of Rome was signed does not exist. Surveys suggest that almost all businessmen in the market countries believe that the existence of the EEC has helped them, and Mr Heath's Government insists that it will help Britain, too. This may be so. But we won't see a 'United States of Europe', as originally envisaged, in the seventies, and may not even see it by the end of the century. (See COMMON MARKET.)

## TRUSTEE SAVINGS BANK

A curious hybrid, half-way between the commercial banks and the National Savings Bank. Its operations are non-profit making and almost every move it makes needs Government approval. There are seventy-five or thereabouts, and their depositors are guaranteed their funds by the Government. The emphasis is much more on savings than on banking, but the mood is swiftly changing. You can open a cheque account similar to a commercial bank current account, and most Trustee Savings Banks will offer many of the services available from their better-known rivals. A TSB account is cheaper to run than a clearing bank account, but there is one major disadvantage – you can't run up an overdraft.

## TRUSTEE STATUS

An accolade much valued by public companies (and organizations like building societies) who care about their standing among investors. It's only when a share has this qualification that it is regarded as 'grown up' and readily accepted in the City. To get trustee status a company has to meet three tests. First it has to have an issued share capital of £1 million. Secondly, it must have paid a dividend on all its issued shares for five consecutive years. Thirdly, its shares must be quoted on a recognized Stock Exchange. These are not onerous qualifications, but trustee status will be quickly revoked should a company miss a dividend payment for one reason or another, during any subsequent twelve months' period. If that happens, it will have to wait a full five years before the shares again become eligible. Trustee status will also be lost if at any time the share capital is reduced to less than £1 million.

Shares with trustee rating have been known to come unstuck, but the casualty rate is comparatively low. It makes them a good first choice for new investors. The shares to concentrate on, though, are not those which have had trustee status for years but those which have only recently acquired it. They are usually more keen to prove that they deserve their admission to the club.

## TUC

Trades Union Congress, the central coordinating body of the

189

trade union movement and its official spokesman. Widely believed to be all-powerful – an impression fostered by all sorts of people, notably TV. Its General Secretary, currently Victor Feather, appears regularly on the small screen, warning the Government, pronouncing judgment on the gold reserves, and talking mournfully about economic growth. He looks and sounds like a man in control, but the reality is different. The TUC has little power to discipline its members, and the General Secretary is much less than the conductor of an orchestra. He is a hired hand who can be overruled by the first violins – the general secretaries of the engineers and the transport workers – if he oversteps the line they lay down. Members quite often defy his edicts. When George Woodcock became General Secretary, in 1960, he was determined to create a new, simple trade union structure more appropriate to modern industrial conditions. He failed and retired nine years later, sadly disillusioned. In Mr Feather's time, we have had incidents like the one-day strikes in protest against the Conservative Government's Industrial Relations Bill – strikes called despite the express disapproval of the TUC.

The TUC's weakness was one of the major reasons why the Tories decided to create a new framework for industrial relations. They radically altered the legal background to the management of labour and the operation of trade unions and employers' organizations. The TUC, predictably, opposed the bill.

Once a year, members meet and debate a number of resolutions. The outcome is decided by the block votes of the big unions; it is they who make policy. Congress makes delegates feel important, but no one else ever takes much notice. 'Unions exist', says the TUC, 'because of the free and spontaneous choice of working people. Their purposes and practices are continually subject to the wishes of the membership through a process of democratic choice.' In short, the TUC does as it is told. The people who do the telling are not necessarily the rank and file: as a rule, they are the more militant and noisy element of the trade union movement. The General Secretary is an Emperor without clothes; he can plead, but he cannot command.

## TURNOVER
The value, or volume, of total sales in any one year. Don't make the

mistake of confusing it with profit. Some companies publish very impressive turnover figures, and innocent investors have been known to jump to the wrong conclusion. A high turnover isn't much good if you don't make any money on it.

The rate at which goods are sold, or 'turned over', is clearly much faster in some areas than in others. Food retailing, for example, tends to see a rapid rate of 'stock turn' at small profit margins. The furniture department of a big store, on the other hand, operates at a much more leisurely pace. It means considerable capital is locked up in stock – but, against this, profit margins tend to be substantially higher. Turnover figures help to show how a company is doing, but they are only a part of the overall picture and therefore need to be approached with caution.

## UNIT TRUSTS

A means of spreading one's risk when investing in stocks and shares. At least, that's the idea. If you have limited savings, and put them all into an account with a respectable bank or building society, you need have no fear. But most people feel the urge to do better: they are more interested in capital gain than a regular, but fixed, rate of interest. Unit Trust is a British term; in America, the equivalent is a Mutual Fund. Both operate on the same basic principle. They sell you shares in their operation, and in turn they employ experts to invest the money in a wide range of business concerns. If these investments rise in value, this is reflected in the value of each share in the fund. And the fund undertakes to redeem a customer's share, at any time, for cash.

The idea is so simple, and the attractions appear so obvious, that mutual funds – and unit trusts – have enjoyed enormous popularity over the years. Many have done well for their clients, but experience has also highlighted the need for caution. One of the first lessons people tend to learn is that markets can go down as well as up. It may seem an easy enough point to grasp, but it's amazing how many newcomers think that capital gains are more or less guaranteed. Another lesson is that mutual fund operators are not in the business for their health; their charges can be substantial and there's no certainty that their investment skill matches their flair for salesmanship. But the most important lesson is that the mutual fund concept is open to abuse. Clients' money may, for example, be used to finance reckless speculation, or to further the interests of directors rather than investors. The Securities and Exchange Commission in America, and the Stock Exchange Council and Board of Trade in Britain, have all kinds of regulations and try to keep a close watch on mutual fund and unit trust activities. But their efforts are not always enough – as the example of Bernard Cornfeld and IOS demonstrated only too well.

Cornfeld made his biggest mark in a variation of the mutual fund idea called the 'offshore fund'. This is, basically, a means of taking large-scale advantage of tax and other financial loopholes in different countries around the world, notably places like the Bahamas, Bermuda, Panama, Liberia, Liechtenstein and Luxemburg. Cornfeld's companies avoided the regulations of markets like Wall Street and London, but in the process also got around almost all the controls designed to prevent speculation getting out of hand. The Cornfeld empire collapsed in 1970, and although there are still plenty of offshore funds in operation, investors have developed a healthy scepticism towards this type of venture. (See also PROPERTY BOND.)

## VALUE-ADDED-TAX
Invented by the French, way back in 1954, as an effective and relatively painless way of taxing goods and services. Britain is switching over to it from April, 1973, and the US administration is said to be 'weighing the pros and cons'.

Instead of covering some goods at high rates, like purchase tax, and some services through a clumsy device like the Selective Employment Tax, VAT will be paid on virtually everything bought and sold. The revenue raised will thus be very large. The same result could be achieved by a straight sales tax, but experience shows that, except when rates are tiny, there is a considerable amount of fraud and evasion. VAT was therefore devised as a way of collecting the money by instalments – a little bit from everybody involved in producing each item, as it moves from raw material, or someone's drawing board, through to the final customer.

Suppose the rate is 10%. A producer sells a raw material for 100p to a manufacturer. The tax is 10p. The manufacturer makes something and sells it for 200p to the wholesaler. His profit is 100p so the tax again is 10p. The wholesaler sells it for an extra 50p and the retailer sells it to the customer after adding on another 50p. They each pay 5p in tax. The consumer pays 330p of which 300p is the cost of the final product and 30p is tax.

The consumer, clearly, bears the brunt of VAT. The actual payment, though, is made by each of the others involved in the process. Critics say it will call for a considerable increase in the number of civil servants, and in the amount of paperwork done by businessmen. They also fear that it will push up the cost of living. Supporters of VAT counter that it will boost productivity, widen the range of indirect taxation, and help exports. Whatever the arguments, VAT is here to stay.

## VENTURE CAPITAL

Finance for young developing firms in areas of high technology. Most 'venture capitalists' – usually bankers with access to institutional funds – tend towards a rather broader view, embracing more or less any company up to the stage of flotation. The basic idea is simple: find a promising small firm, provide financial backing, and share in its success. The risks implicit in venture capital are considerably higher than those associated with more conventional forms of investment, which is why the more staid finance houses don't care for it. Many venture capital companies have failed, costing their backers large sums of money.

In the United States, where the concept of twentieth-century venture capital first developed, even the oldest and probably the most successful practitioner, American Research and Development, has barely kept pace with the Dow-Jones index since the war. That was largely because it backed a company, Digital Equipment Corporation, which has shown a huge increase on the original investment. In Britain, the famous Rothschild merchant banking house has tried its hand with notable lack of success. One reason may be that European merchant banks are too much bankers and not enough industrialists; venture capital situations often have to be

G

made to work through the guidance of a central management service
rather than left to their own devices.

## VICIOUS CIRCLE
Action and reaction that intensify each other in a harmful way. Inflation, for example, will usually lead to more inflation – because
workers, in order to make up for higher prices, will use their bargaining power to get more money, which in turn will force employers to put up prices yet again. Poor countries, too, tend to be
caught up in a vicious circle: they don't make adequate use of
resources, and because they don't make adequate use of resources
they cannot provide investment for further development, and because they cannot provide investment for further development they
continue to make inadequate use of resources. If you see what I
mean.

## WASTING ASSETS
Anything which in the foreseeable future will need to be replaced
or taken out of use because it has become worn out or obsolete. A
lease on a house is a 'wasting asset'. In industry, the term mostly
refers to plant, machinery and equipment – though it could be
applied just as easily to people, including the managing director. It
is an accepted principle that, in the accounts, wasting assets should
be written down in value over their working life so that, subject to
any residual or scrap value they may finally possess, the capital outlay at the time of purchase is recovered out of the profits earned. The
amounts written off each year are known as 'depreciation'.

## WEALTH TAX
We already have taxes on inherited wealth, in the form of death
duties, and taxes on capital gains made through investments in one's
lifetime. The idea behind a wealth tax is that someone should, from
time to time, measure our total worth and charge us a percentage on
it. It's done in a number of other countries, including West Germany and Sweden, and is very much part of socialist philosophy.
There are, however, several snags. The first is to decide just exactly
what to regard as 'wealth'. In the early sixties, the word was applied

to assets worth more than £20,000. Rapid inflation, however, has made that figure look very modest. The problem is easily solved by raising the starting point. The second snag is much more serious: how do you prevent widespread evasion? The two Labour Chancellors who held office between 1964 and 1970 both investigated the possibility of introducing a wealth tax, and rejected the idea on the grounds that collecting it would be too troublesome. But it will almost certainly be revived in future election manifestoes.

## WIDER BANDS

As a rule, each country's paper money has a fixed value in terms of other currencies. But, of course, there are bound to be fluctuations. So there is usually a margin, a range, or as the jargon has it, a band. The deal agreed between Common Market countries in 1972, is, perhaps, a good example. Under it, Common Market currencies – the mark, the franc, the lira, the guilder and so on – are allowed to fluctuate against each other by no more than 2·25%. In other words, they can rise or fall by that amount before official efforts are made to keep them stable. This is a rather narrower range of fluctuation than most other countries permit, and the Common Market system was dubbed the 'snake in the tunnel' of the 'wider bands' accepted outside the Market. The reason is simple: it's important for everyone to know where he stands, not only because it makes trade easier but because so many Common Market schemes – such as the agricultural policy – would otherwise be in trouble. Some countries, though, are very reluctant to accept what amounts, in effect, to a monetary straitjacket. This is why one so often hears talk of the need for wider bands, or 'exchange rate flexibility'. Britain, although committed to joining the Market, brushed aside the EEC deal when it decided to float the pound in 1972. (See FLOATING, FIXED PARITY and DEVALUATION.)

## WINDING UP

Also known as liquidation. Whereas bankruptcy is a personal thing, to be applied only to an individual, winding up applies only to corporations. It is the process by which a limited liability company ends its legal existence. This may happen because the reason for its existence has gone: a company which had sold all its assets would clearly have no reason to remain in being. But the most common cause for winding up is that the directors are no longer able to pay their creditors.

There are two basic forms of liquidation – voluntary and compulsory. The first is possible only if the company can pay its debts within the next twelve months. Compulsory winding up is undergone for a variety of reasons, but the main one is insolvency.

What generally happens is that a creditor, or group of creditors, presents a petition to the court. At the hearing a winding up order is made and a liquidator is appointed on a temporary basis. At this stage, he is usually the Official Receiver – an officer of the Department of Trade and Industry who is also an officer of the Court. A statement of affairs is filed within fourteen days of a winding-up order, and the official receiver reports to the court. A meeting of creditors is held, at which the liquidator is confirmed or a new one appointed. He collects all the assets, and creditors are paid off either in full or at so-and-so-much in the pound. The winding up is then completed. This, of course, is only a brief outline of what often proves to be a complex and disputatious procedure: liquidation is seldom a pleasant business.

## WISE MEN
Any group of people asked by governments to find out where we're going, or to study the implications of some particular scheme. A journalistic term, designed to impress readers with the importance of the team. The 'wise men' are often economists, and their reports tend to be weighty documents. The results, alas, are usually less impressive. 'Many a crown of wisdom', American poet Paul Eldridge once said, 'is but the golden chamberpot of success, worn with pompous dignity.' Yes.

## WORKERS' CONTROL
A popular concept, based on the unshakeable conviction that all would be well if only management would step aside and let shop stewards have a go. In Britain, the notion goes back to the industrial revolution. There have been quite a number of experiments, and

196

nearly all of them have failed. For as a rule, it simply reflects a determined refusal to face unpalatable financial facts. Never mind if a factory cannot sell the stuff it makes: production must be maintained regardless. The state can be relied upon to foot the bill.

There would be a great deal less enthusiasm for the idea if one suggested that workers should run, say, the coal industry as an independent, unsubsidized operation. There is nothing to stop the unions, with their millions in stocks and shares, taking over an industrial company and showing the world that they can, indeed, do better. But it does not suit them to do so. One very good reason is that the present system gives them far more effective 'control': union strength is such that few managements dare brush aside the shop stewards' wishes. Another is that the workers themselves are sceptical; they are less interested in idealism than in the financial backing for their weekly pay packets. It suits them to have bosses to complain to, and to have shop stewards complain on their behalf. They don't want to be their own bosses.

It is even questionable whether the majority of workers are all that keen on nationalization. State ownership very often is a bigger foe than private enterprise. The strength of a skilled worker lies in his ability to swop jobs: state ownership reduces the range of choice.

Some people would, of course, argue that this is only so under a capitalist system. But communism is worse. Officially the worker controls Soviet industry. In practice, he does nothing of the sort. If he works for, say, the railways he finds that, as in Britain, control is firmly in the hands of the managerial class, itself dominated by the Moscow bureaucratic class. Not only is the worker far removed from real power, but the elaborate pretence that industry is being managed in his name deprives him of the right to use his most effective weapon – the strike. It is 'not necessary'. There's a popular Russian joke which asks: 'You know the difference between capitalism and socialism?' Answer: 'Capitalism means exploitation of man by his fellow man. In socialism, it's precisely the other way around . . .'

## WORLD BANK
Perhaps the most imposing name in banking. Its formal name is The International Bank for Reconstruction and Development,

which is more pompous and long-winded than World Bank but rather less misleading. The Bank's customers are nations and no borrower ever walks away with cash in his pocket.

The World Bank was founded, together with the International Monetary Fund, in the resort town of Bretton Woods. One of its original mandates was to help finance the reconstruction of Europe following World War II, but when the United States established the Marshall Plan the Bank turned to the development side of its task. The Bank and its affiliates have tended to concentrate on financing specific projects in public utilities, transportation, agriculture, industry – and, more recently, education projects, tourism, and family planning. In 1955, the Bank made world headlines when it withdrew from a commitment to help finance the Aswan Dam following pressure from the American and British Governments. The episode is nowadays remembered with some sense of shame; 'we wouldn't do it again', says one senior official.

Originally, the Bank's funds came from the capital subscriptions of its members, whose percentage of ownership is related to their national income and position in world trade. Today it gets its funds mainly from the sale of its bonds in the capital markets of the world and other borrowing, and from the repayment of earlier loans. The bonds are bought by central banks, pension and trust funds, insurance companies and other private investors. Conscious of the need to maintain a high reputation, the Bank keeps a close watch on countries which secure a loan: teams of experts make careful on-the-spot investigations before it parts with any money, and the watch continues once a project is under way.

Left-wing critics say the World Bank is a capitalist tool for 'structuring the global market for private gain'. Bank officials claim it is a development agency dedicated to narrowing the gap between rich and poor. The one is consistent with the other. Ideal or not, the Bank has certainly played a useful role in alleviating hardship.

## YANKEE, GO HOME
Europe's answer to what French author Jean-Jacques Schreiber called 'the American challenge'. Usually found scrawled on walls of American-owned plants, or chanted by militant trade unionists.

Heard most loudly whenever a visiting US industrialist breaks an unwritten rule drummed into every American sent to colonize the industrial wastelands of Europe: beat them, cheat them, outsmart them, but never tell the Europeans what you really think of their goddam methods. Most corporations go out of their way to identify themselves with the 'host country'. They appoint British (or French, or German) directors and, wherever possible, retain the traditional local names. What, you might ask, could be more British than Campbell's soups, British Wire Products, Britannia Lead Company, British Typewriters, and British United Shoe Machinery? They are all owned by Americans.

Economists acknowledge that US investment has done a lot for Britain. It has provided much-needed employment in areas neglected by British companies, and has made a useful contribution to the modernization of British industry. American firms bring not just capital, but new manufacturing processes and the latest management techniques. If the Government were to suppress US investment, it would simply move elsewhere. But why should it? American companies operating here are as much subject to British rules and regulations as everyone else, and their ability to dictate events should not be overrated. Nor should one exaggerate their desire to ride rough-shod over local customs and government policies. But even if they did try to ride roughshod over local customs, should we consider it such a bad thing? Some of our customs deserve no better. And the deeply ingrained European habit of seeing everything in nationalist terms looks increasingly old-fashioned. It has certainly helped the Americans: it is they who leap across frontiers and create powerful multi-national corporations, they who are pushing Europe into the direction it logically ought to go.

## YIELD

The most widely used term in investment; it means, quite simply, the annual return from any individual holding. The normal method is to declare it as a percentage of the nominal value of a share. For example, if a dividend of 10% were paid on shares with a nominal value of £1, each shareholder would get a 'gross' dividend (that is, before tax has been deducted) of ten pence for every share held. The price you have paid for your shares may, of course, differ from the nominal value. So if you want to calculate your real return, multiply the nominal value by the rate of dividend paid, and then divide by the market price.

*The Financial Times* publishes gross dividend yields for a wide list of shares every day. A high yield is usually an indication that the company has an unstable record, or that the market thinks there is a risk of a dividend cut. It is often accompanied by a low 'cover' – a figure which shows the extent to which the profits earned for the ordinary shares were enough to cover the cost of the last dividend payment. A cover of, say, 1·4 times indicates that there is very little margin if things happen to go wrong.

Rubber and tea plantations traditionally offer high yields, because the risks are obviously greater here than in other sections. A share like Marks and Spencer, on the other hand, will invariably show a low yield – perhaps 2–3%. This is because the market has come to expect good things from the share; it is known as a 'growth stock'. Cover is less important, because earnings are likely to go up.

People who depend on the income from their investments are obviously more concerned with yield than those who are chiefly interested in capital gain. The latter may buy a share even if the yield is as low as 1%, because they have reason to think that the company has excellent prospects. Yields ought to be read in conjunction with price-earnings ratios (see page 146) and other yardsticks.

## ZERO GROWTH
Nothing. Nil. No progress of any kind. Trust economists, though, to find a fancy way of saying it.

# Further Reading

There is no shortage of economics textbooks, but most of them are of little use to the layman. Here's a list of books which I personally would recommend to anyone who is put off by excessive use of jargon, but nevertheless wants to take a closer look at economics and finance.

WELCOME TO THE CONGLOMERATE – YOU'RE FIRED!, by Isadore Barmash, Weidenfeld and Nicolson.

WHAT ECONOMICS IS ABOUT, by Michael Barratt Brown, Weidenfeld and Nicolson.

STEERING THE ECONOMY, by Samuel Brittain, Pelican Books.

THE PRICE OF ECONOMIC FREEDOM, by Samuel Brittain, Macmillan.

BUSINESS AS A GAME, by Albert Z. Carr, J. M. Dent.

BRITAIN'S ECONOMIC PROSPECTS, by Richard E. Caves and Associates, George Allen and Unwin.

A POPULAR HISTORY OF TAXATION, by James Coffield, Longmans.

THE AGE OF DISCONTINUITY, by Peter F. Drucker, Pan Books.

THE GNOMES OF ZURICH, by T. R. Fehrenbach, Leslie Frewin.

MEN AND MONEY – Financial Europe Today, by Paul Ferris, Pelican.

THE AFFLUENT SOCIETY, by J. K. Galbraith, Penguin.

THE NEW INDUSTRIAL STATE, by J. K. Galbraith, André Deutsch.

THE WORLD OF GOLD, by Timothy Green, Michael Joseph.

THE NAKED MANAGER, by Robert Heller, Barrie and Jenkins.

WHAT SHALL I DO WITH MY MONEY?, by Eliot Janeway, Michael Joseph.

MANAGEMENT AND MACHIAVELLI, by Antony Jay, Hodder and Stoughton.

THE EXCEPTIONAL EXECUTIVE, by Harry Levinson, Harvard University Press.

PLAYBOY'S INVESTMENT GUIDE, by Michael Lawrence, Playboy Press.

CREDIT CARDMANSHIP, by Martin J. Meyer, Berkeley Publishing Corporation.

THE MANAGERS, Roy Lewis and Rosemary Stewart, New American Library.

THE AMERICAN TAKE-OVER OF BRITAIN, by James MacMillan and Bernard Harris, Leslie Frewin.

21 POPULAR ECONOMIC FALLACIES, by E. J. Mishan, Pelican Books.

A HISTORY OF MONEY, by E. V. Morgan, Pelican Books.

FURTHER READING

GREAT MYTHS OF ECONOMICS, by Don Paarlberg, New American Library.

DO YOU SINCERELY WANT TO BE RICH ?, by Charles Raw, Bruce Page and Godfrey Hodgson, André Deutsch.

DO IT THE HARD WAY, by Keith Richardson, Weidenfeld and Nicolson.

ANATOMY OF EUROPE, by Anthony Sampson, Hodder and Stoughton.

THE MONEY GAME, by Adam Smith, Michael Joseph and Pan Books.

CORPORATIONS IN CRISIS, by Richard Austen Smith, Doubleday and Co.

UP THE ORGANISATION, by Robert Townsend, Michael Joseph.

NOTHING CERTAIN BUT TAX, by John Turing, Hodder and Stoughton.

THE MERCHANT BANKERS, by Joseph Wechsberg, Weidenfeld & Nicolson.

THE POUND IN YOUR POCKET, 1870-1970, by Peter Wilsher, Cassell.

FONTANA INTRODUCTION TO MODERN ECONOMICS, seven books each by a different economist.

... and my own two books: THREE YEARS HARD LABOUR (André Deutsch) and MERGER MANIA (Constable).

# Index

# INDEX